The GRUMPY Doodle Book

Taro Gomi

chronicle books · san francisco

I don't know what you're grumpy about, but why don't you try doodling? Doodle anything you like. See? Aren't you starting to feel better?

What kind of face do you make when you're grumpy?

Let's draw a person being very cranky inside this house.

Let’s draw an angry teapot.

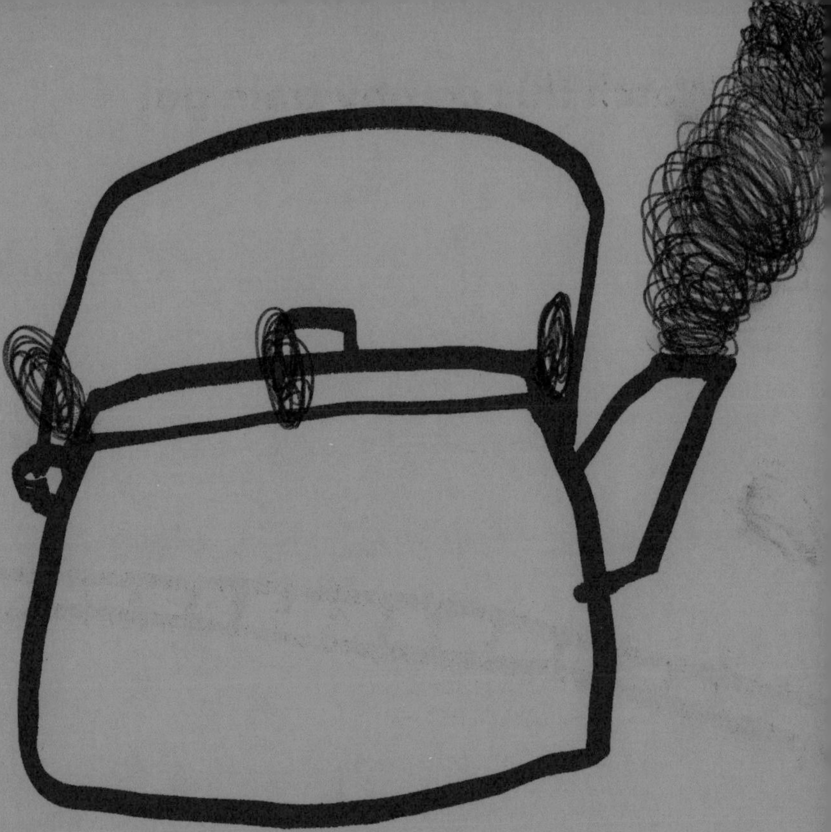

Watch this crabby train go!

What do grouchy mountains look like?

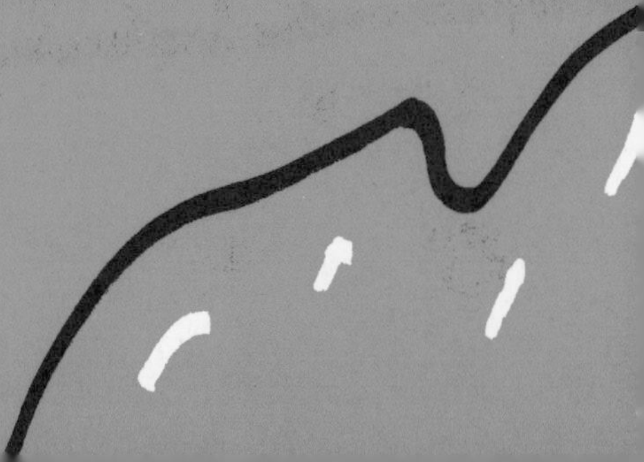

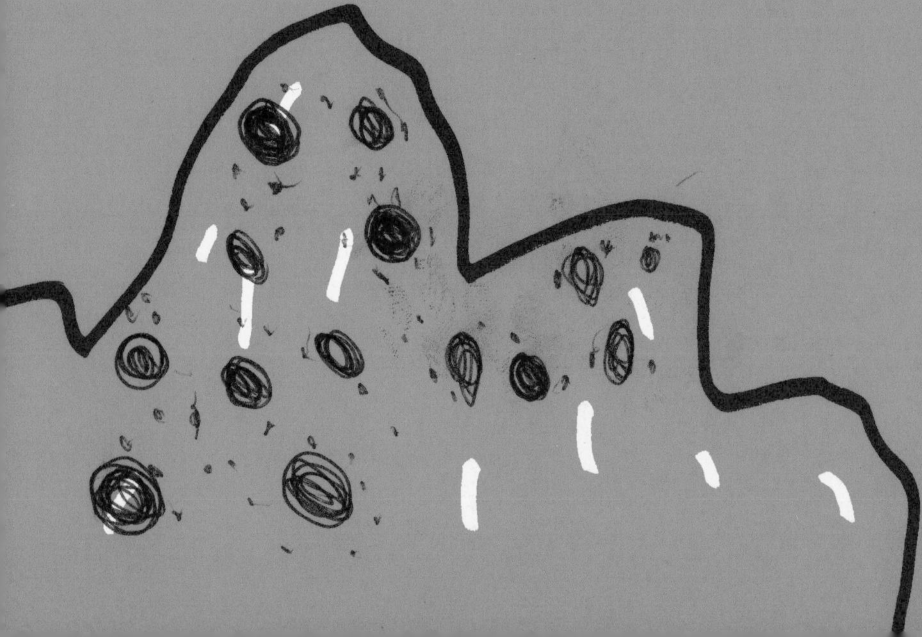

Let's draw a peevish snowman.

Let's angrily write the letter **A**.

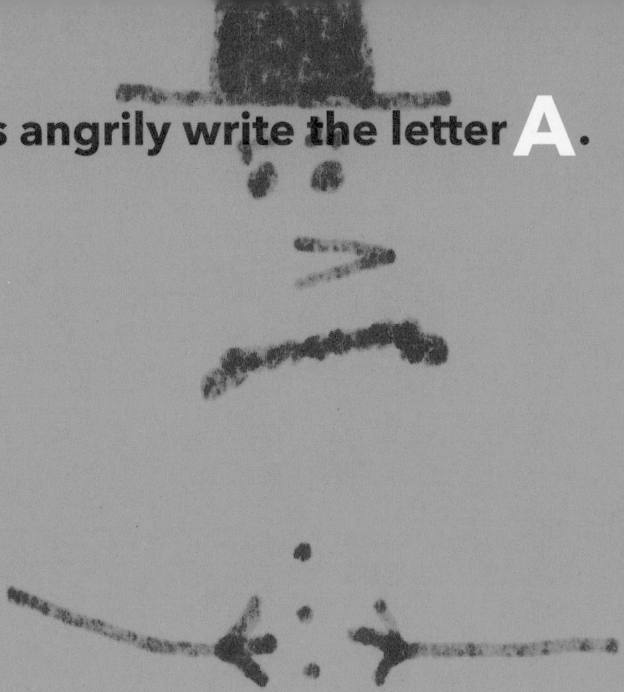

What kind of clothes do you wear when you're feeling mad?

Let's draw a person irritably riding a bike.

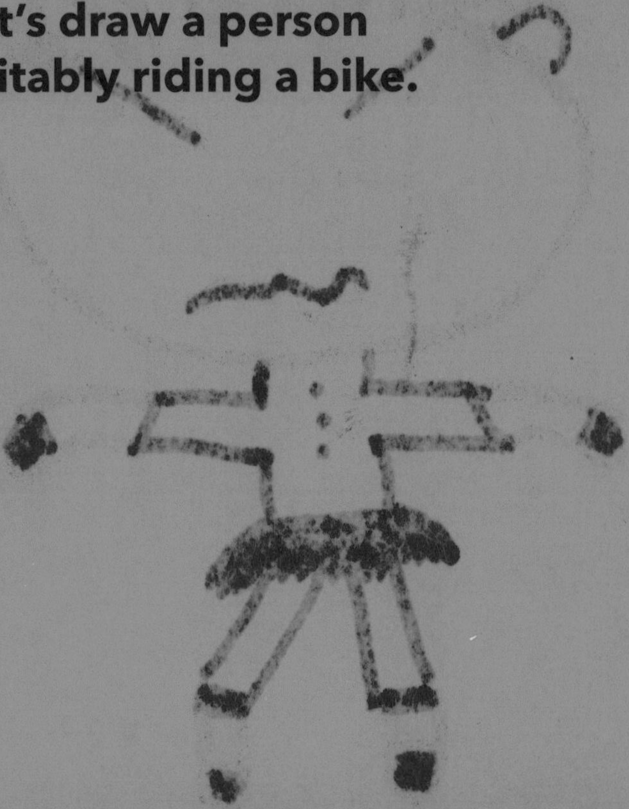

Sloth

What time is it on this furious clock?

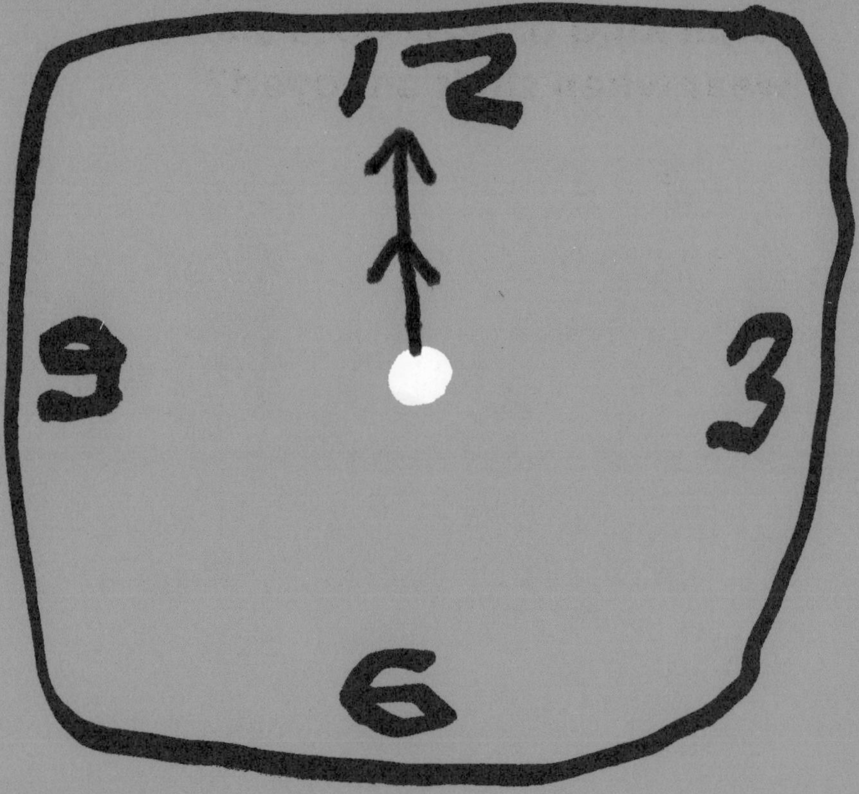
12
9
3
6

What kind of bow does she wear when she's annoyed?

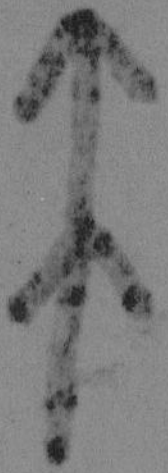

Let's draw a person angrily kicking the ball.

Let’s draw a very crabby ocean.

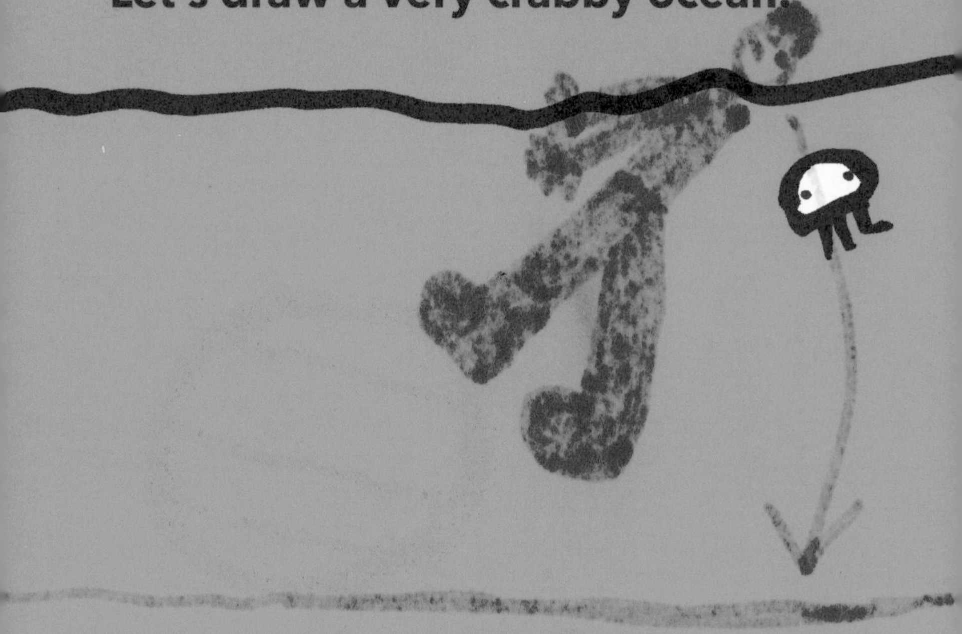

Let’s draw a bird angrily flying.

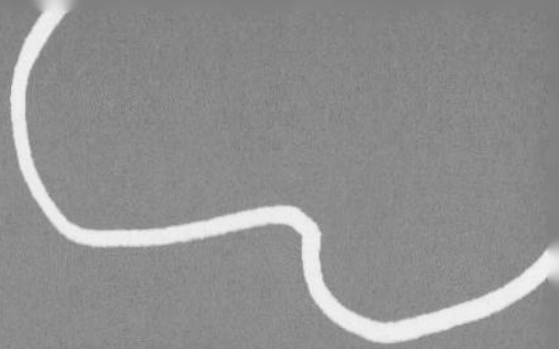

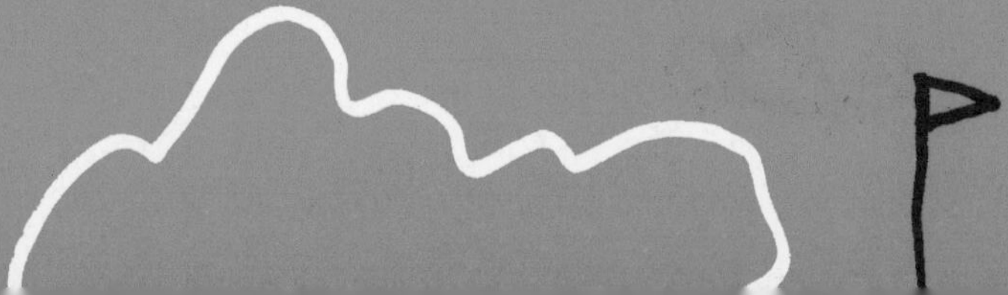

Let's draw a cranky scarecrow.

Look! A very irritated bug is coming this way.

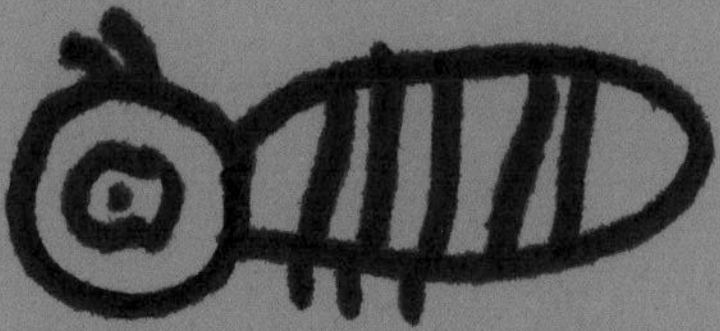

It's the god of thunder. He's always in a bad mood!

What kind of umbrella does a grumpy person carry?

What does an aggravated doll look like?

Let’s make these squiggles more and more tangled.

Let’s make these bookshelves messier and messier.

Let's calm down a bit and do some math.

$$\begin{array}{r} 305 \\ +\quad 2 \\ \hline 527 \end{array}$$

Now draw a furious-looking man!

Let's draw an angry-looking woman.

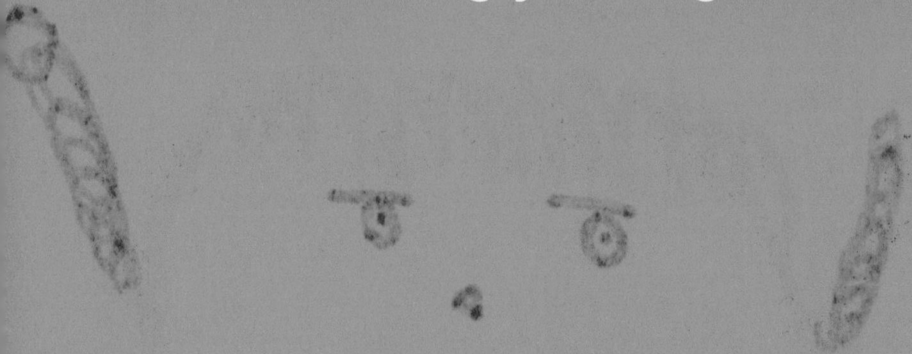

Well, well! You don't look grumpy anymore. What does your face look like now? Now that you're feeling better, turn the page for more doodling.

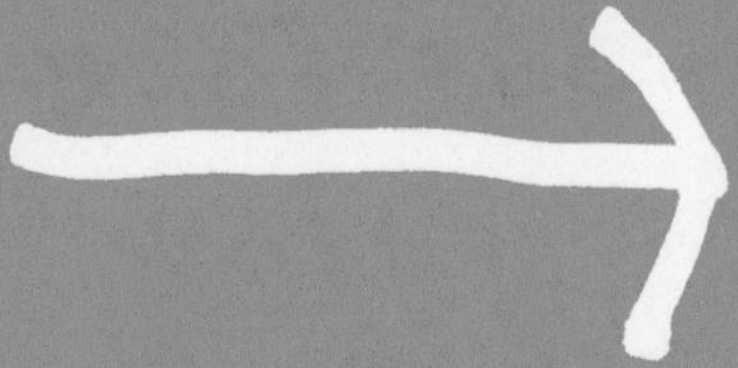

118 r15

6)713

−6

11

−6

53

−48

15

222

3)666

−6

06

−6

06

−6

0

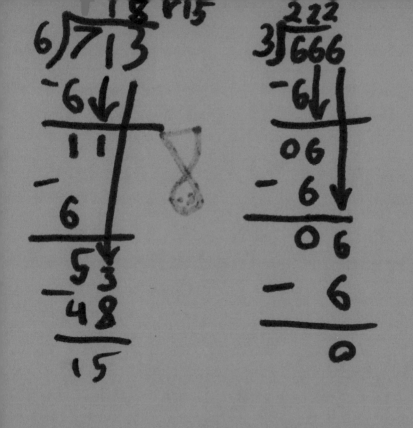

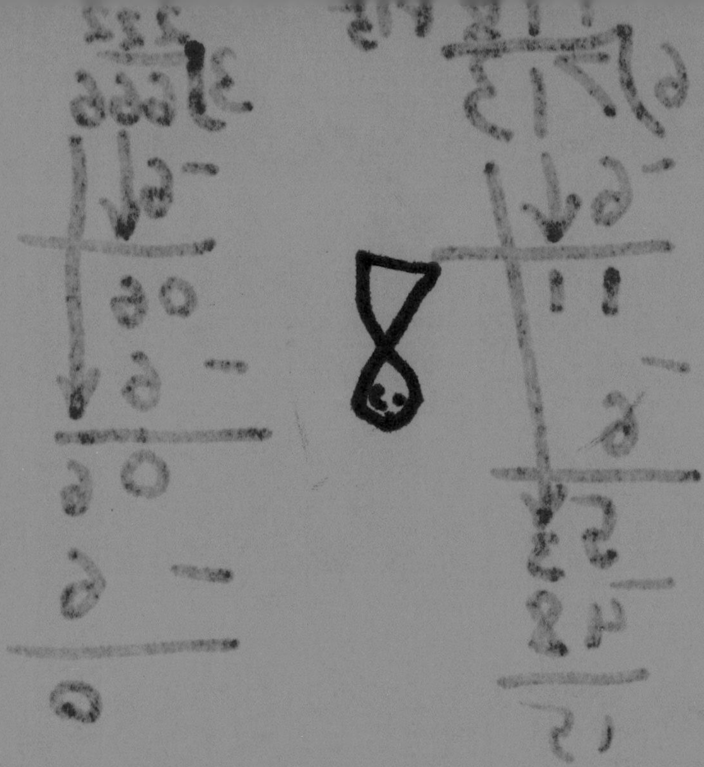

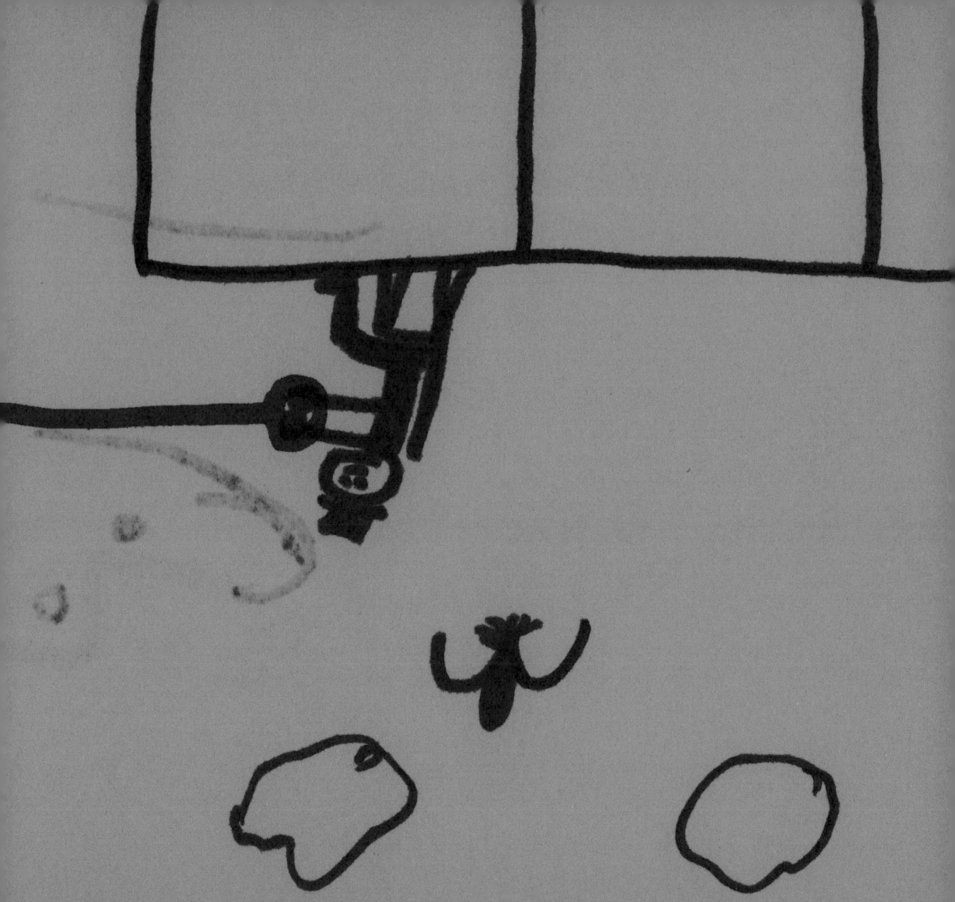

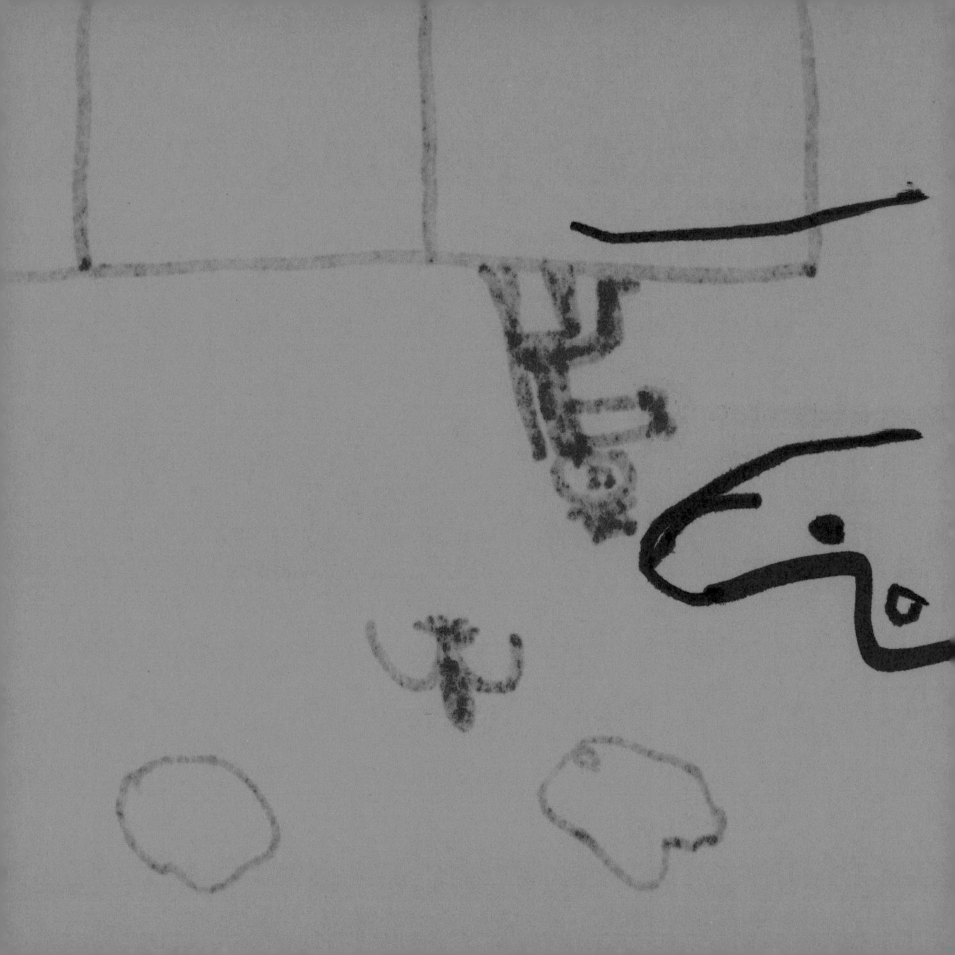

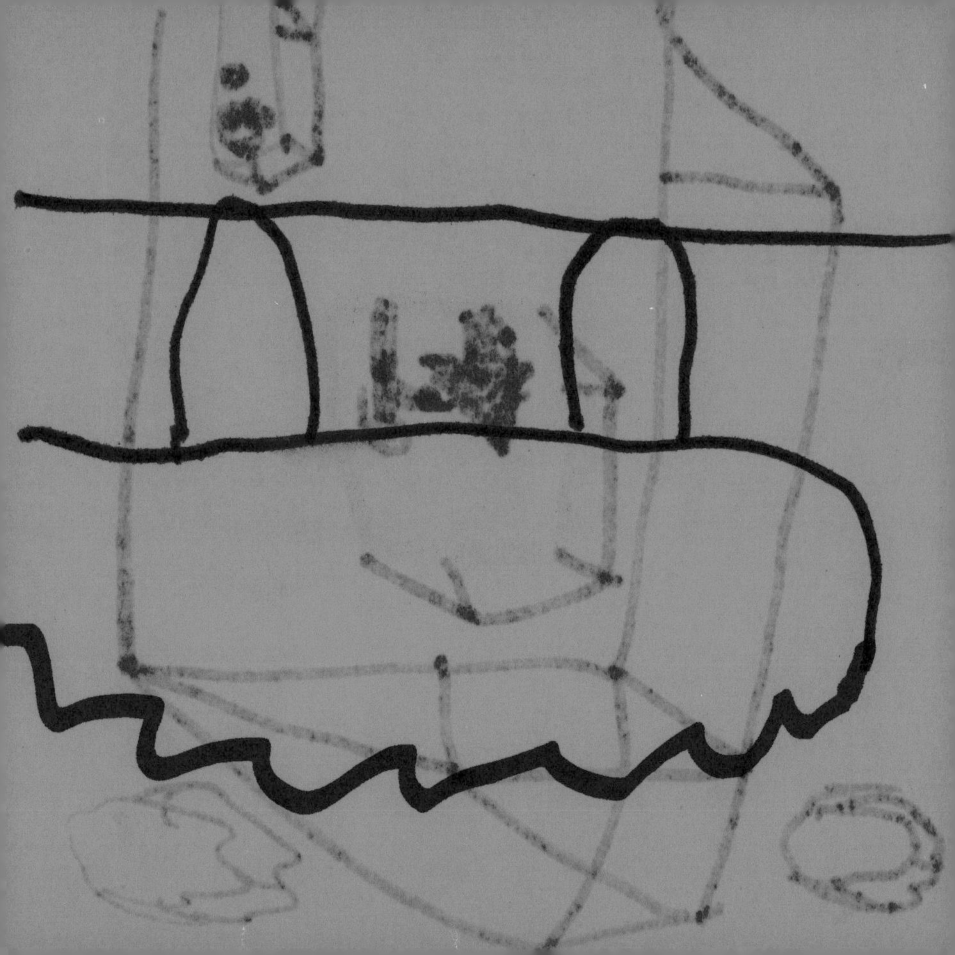

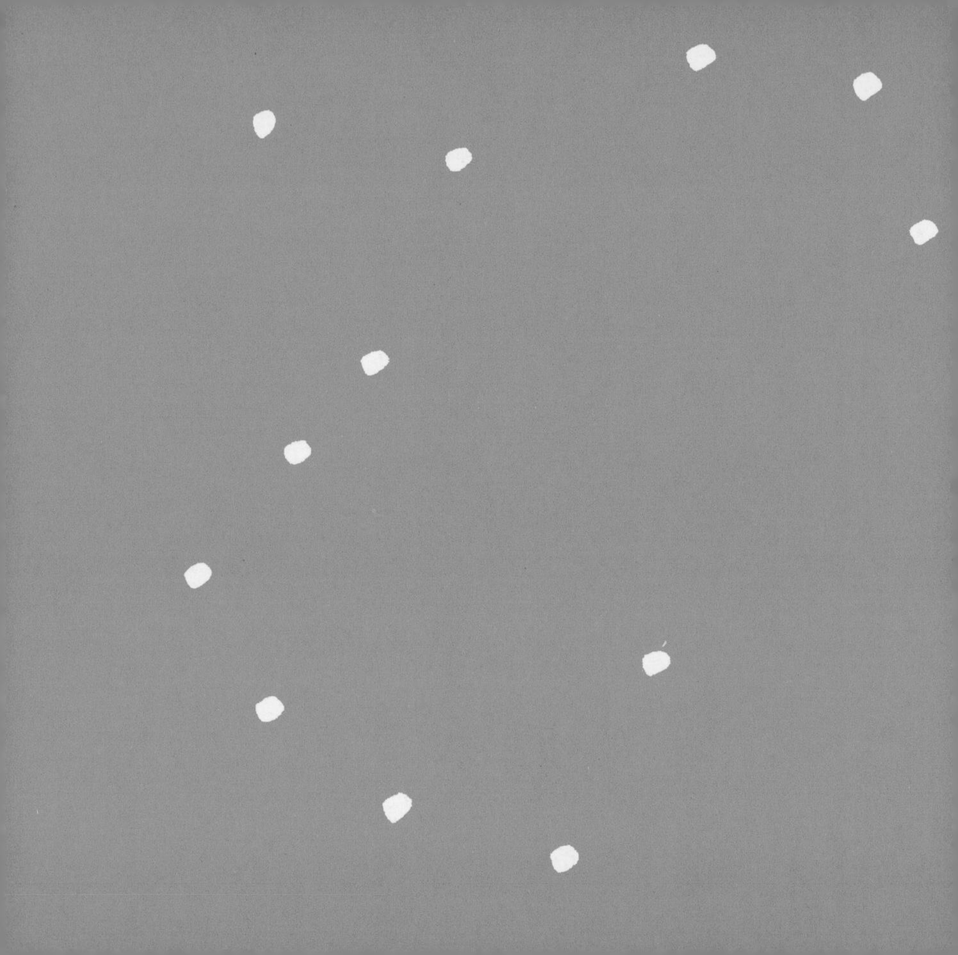

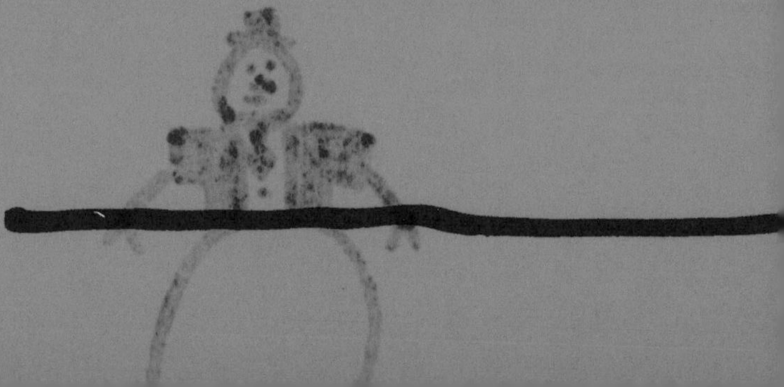

```
   135 r4
5)679
 -5↓
  17
 -15↓
   29
 - 25
   4
```

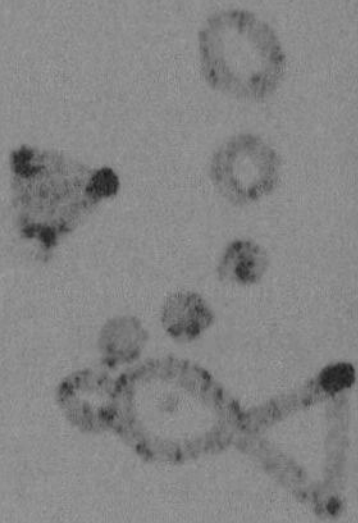

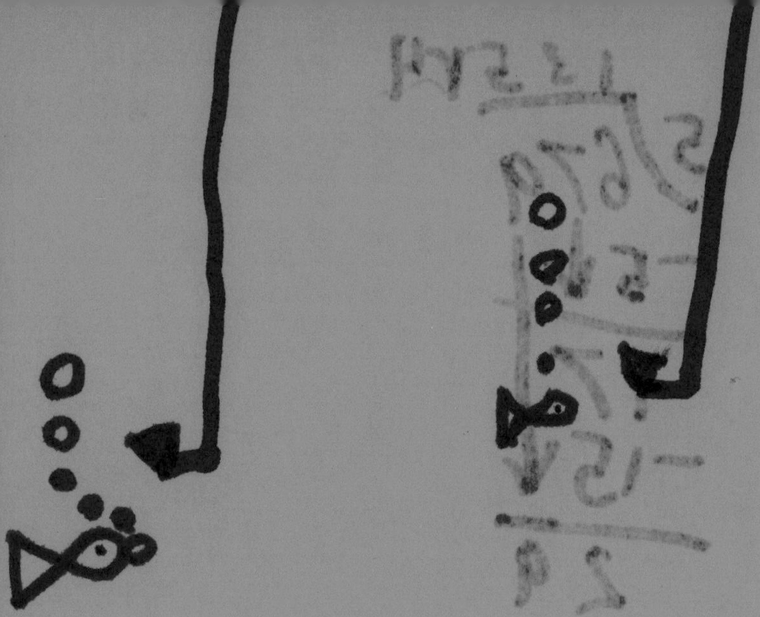

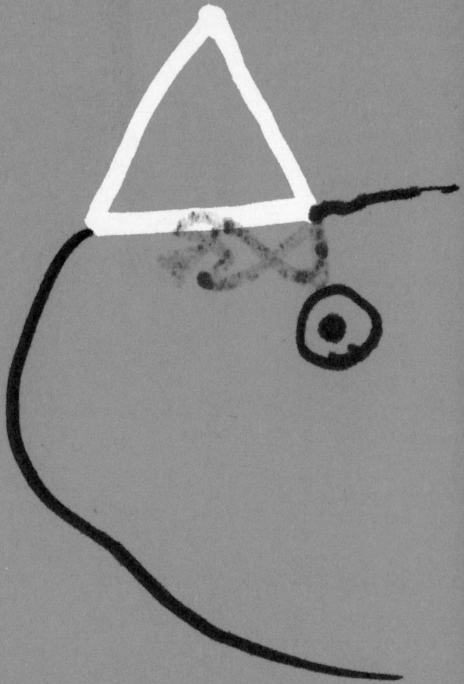

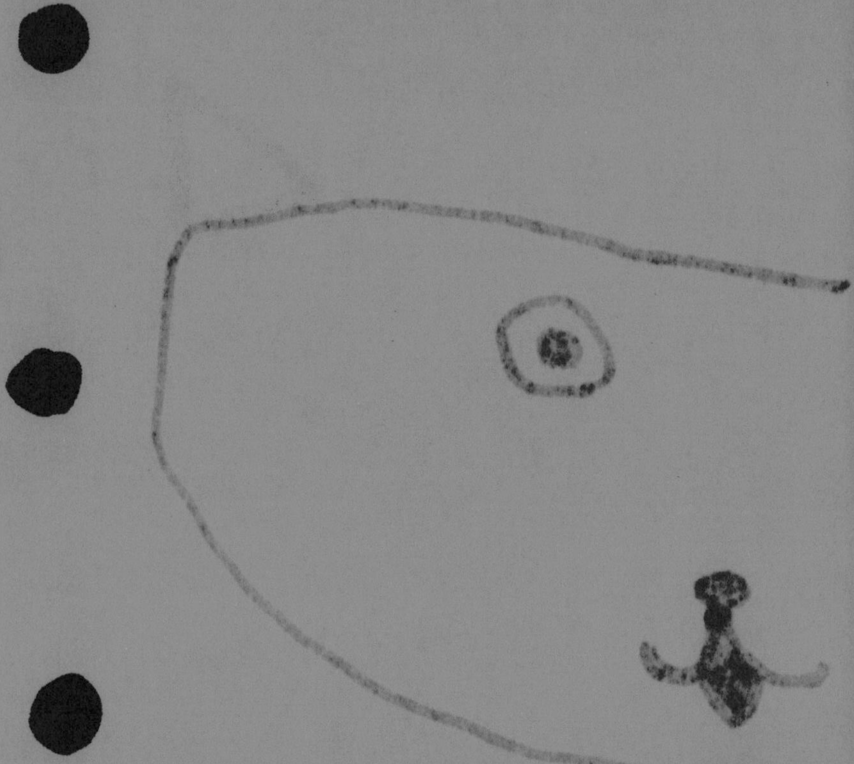

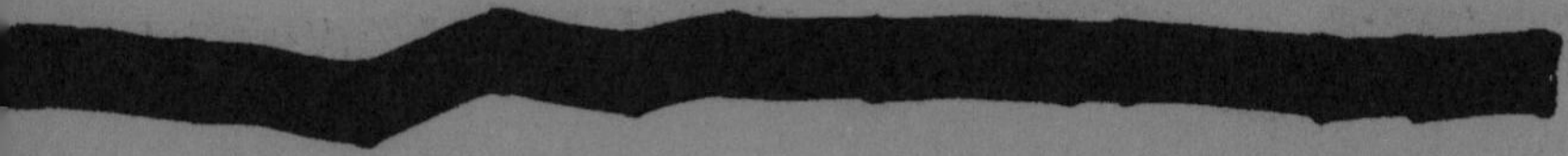

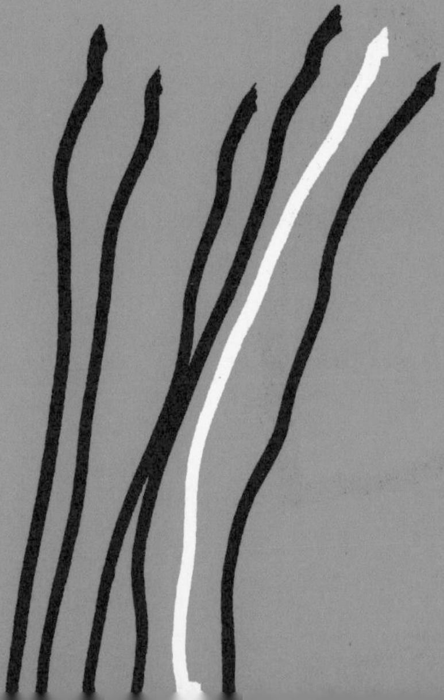

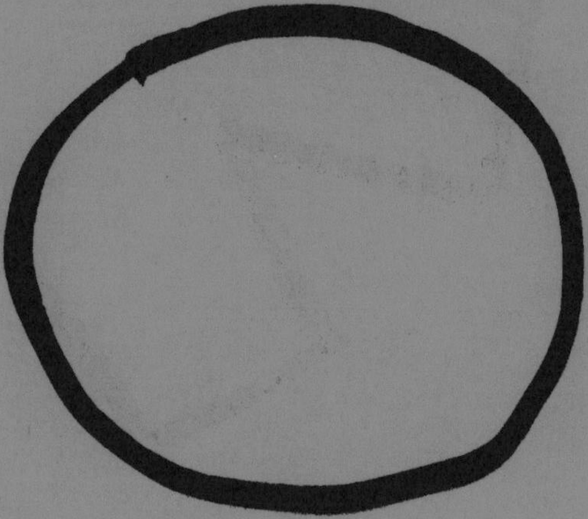

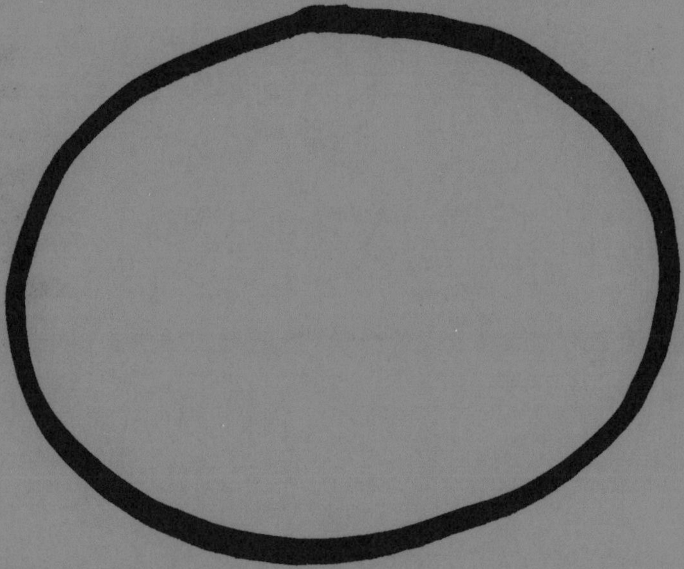

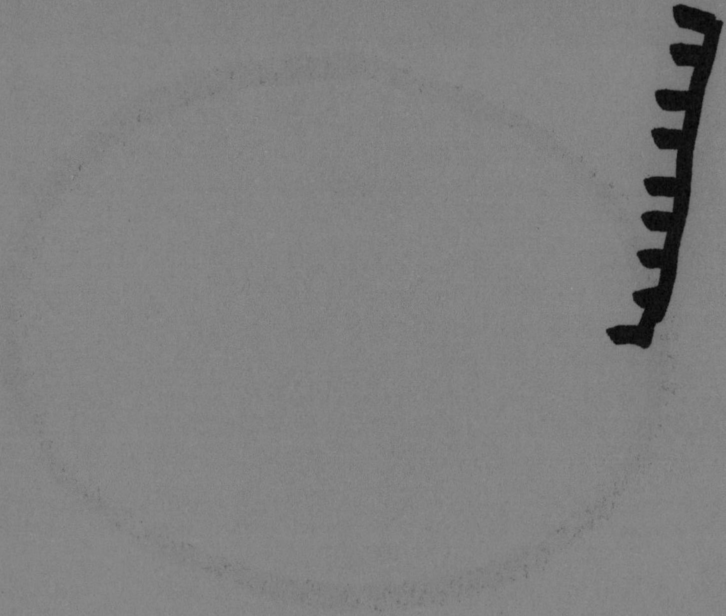

T

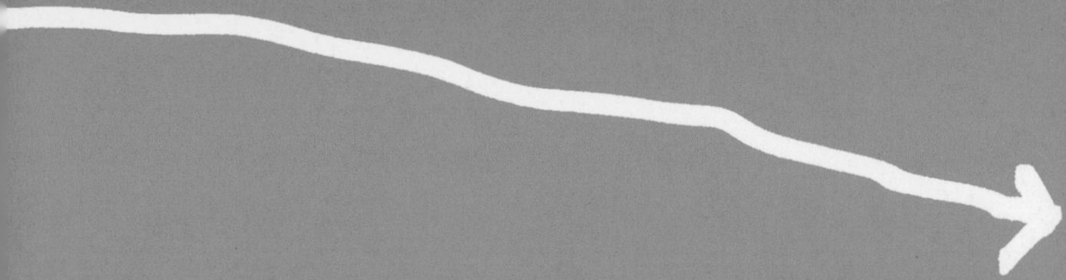

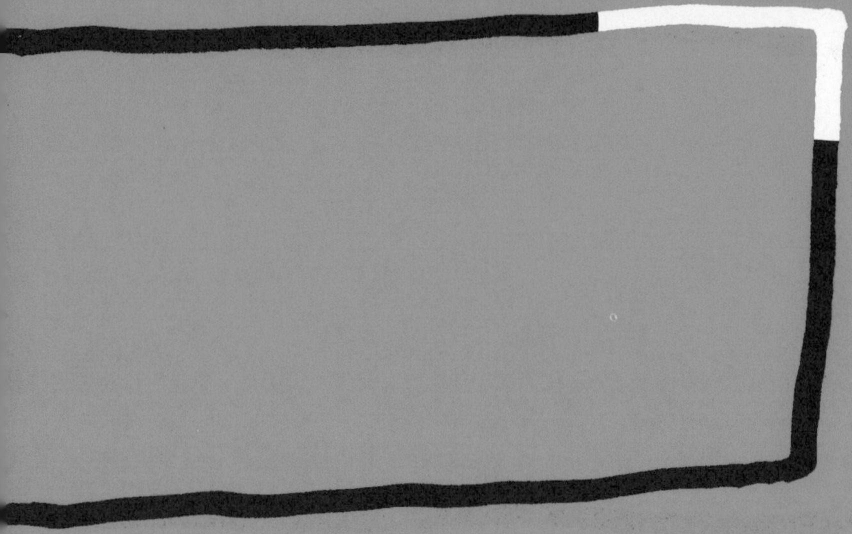

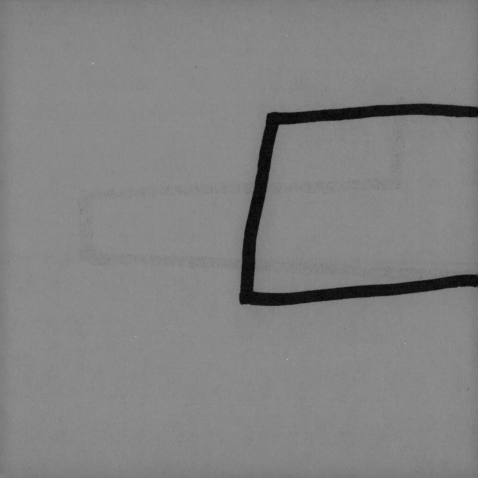

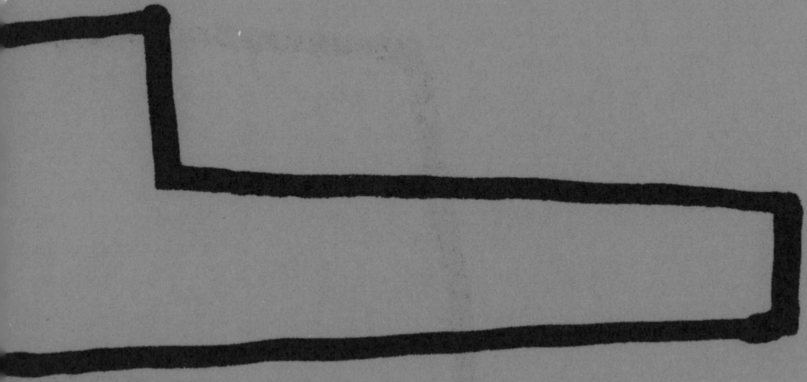

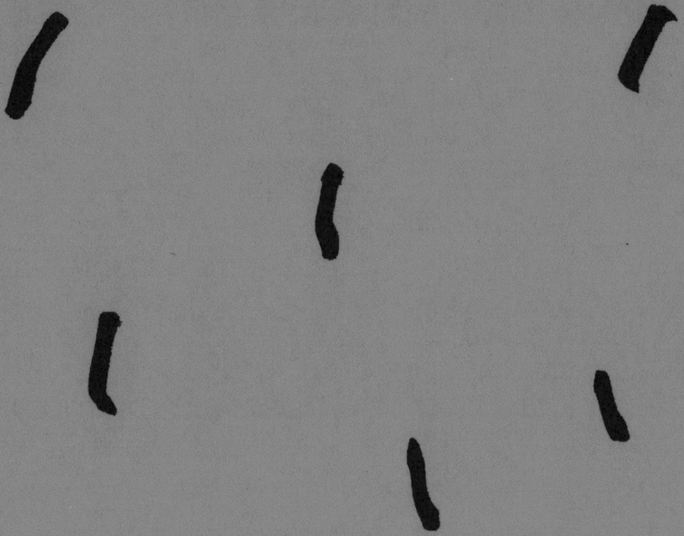

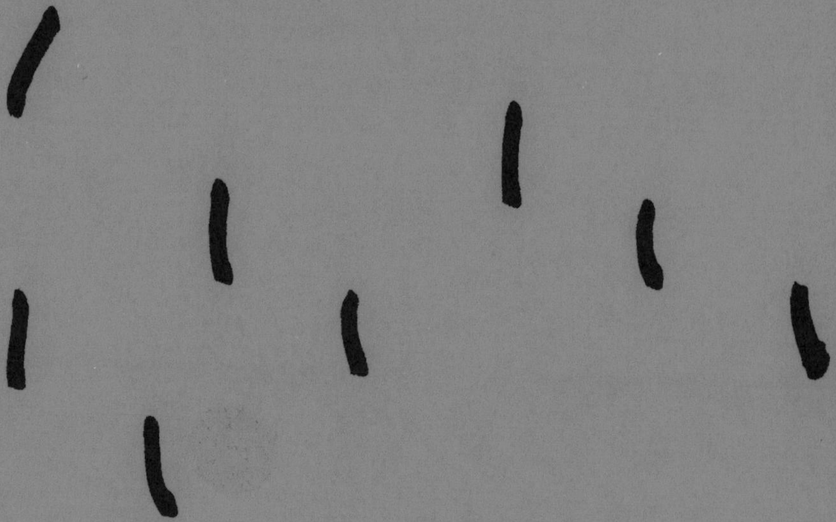

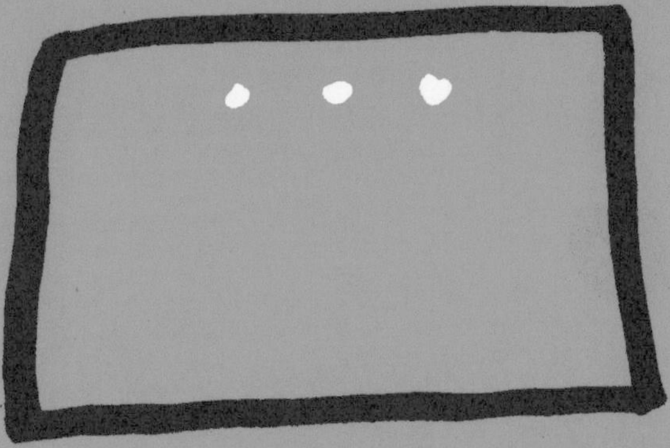

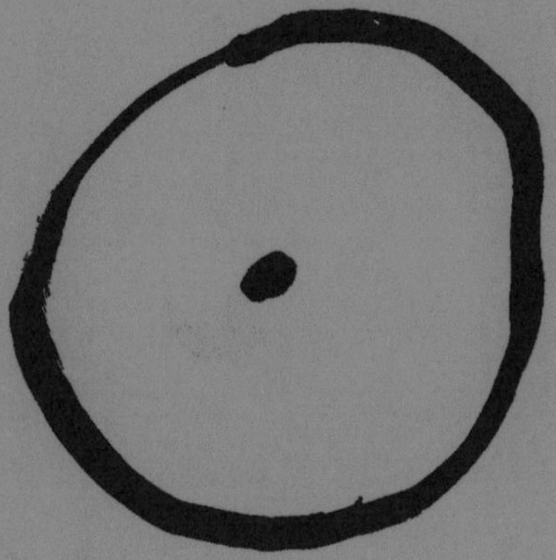

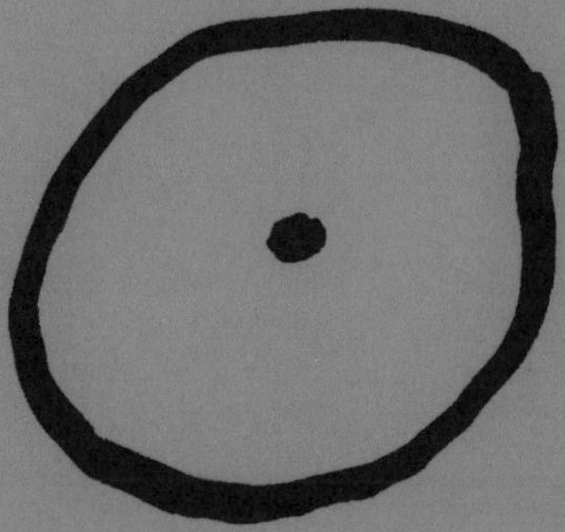

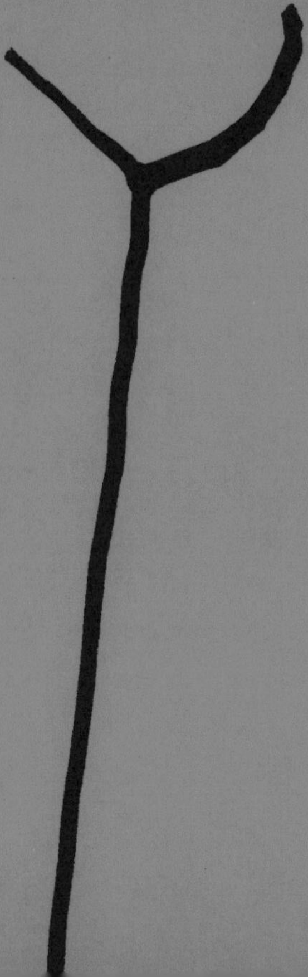

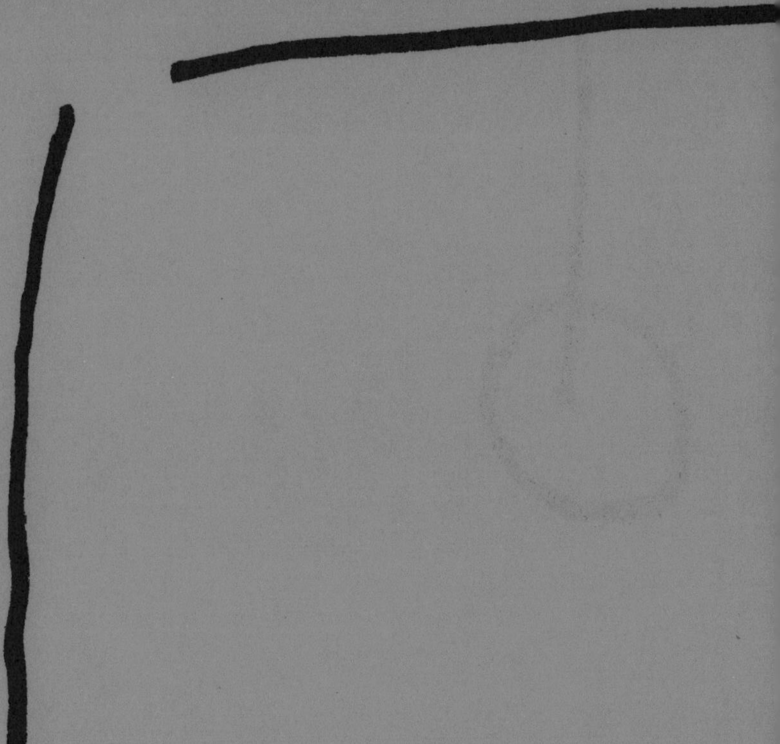

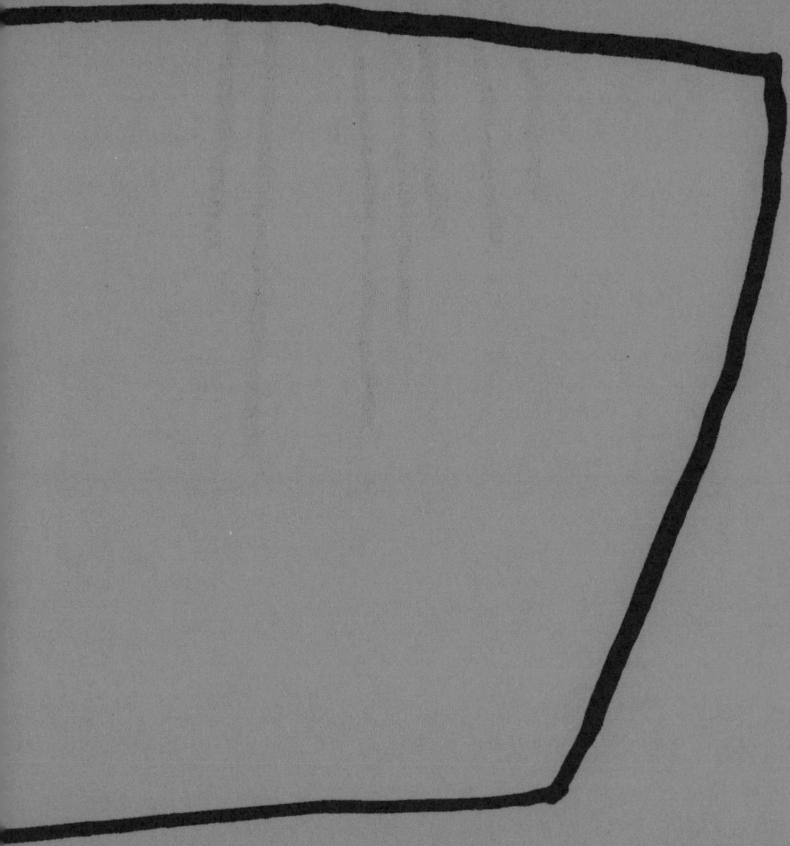

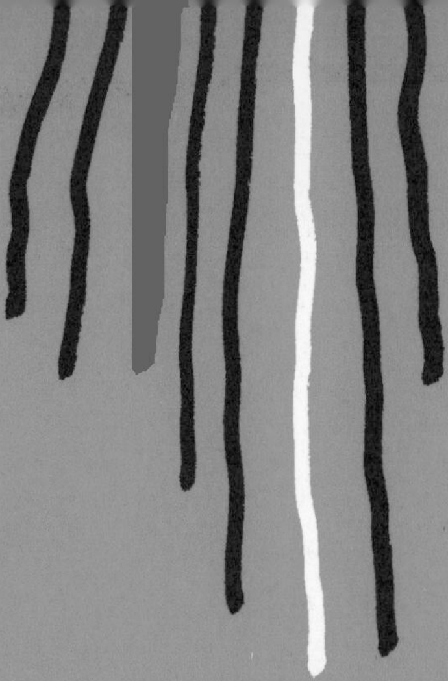

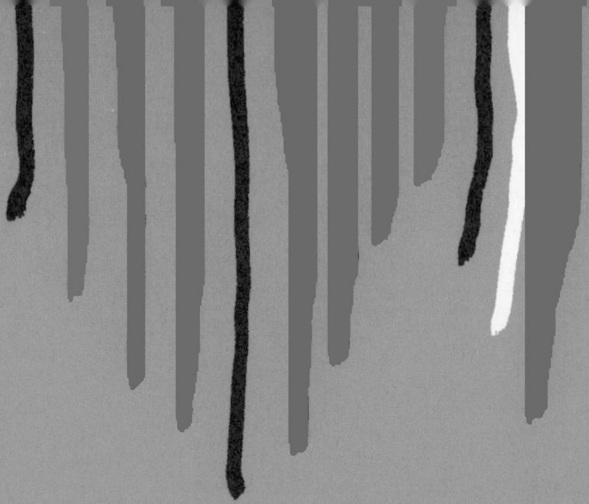

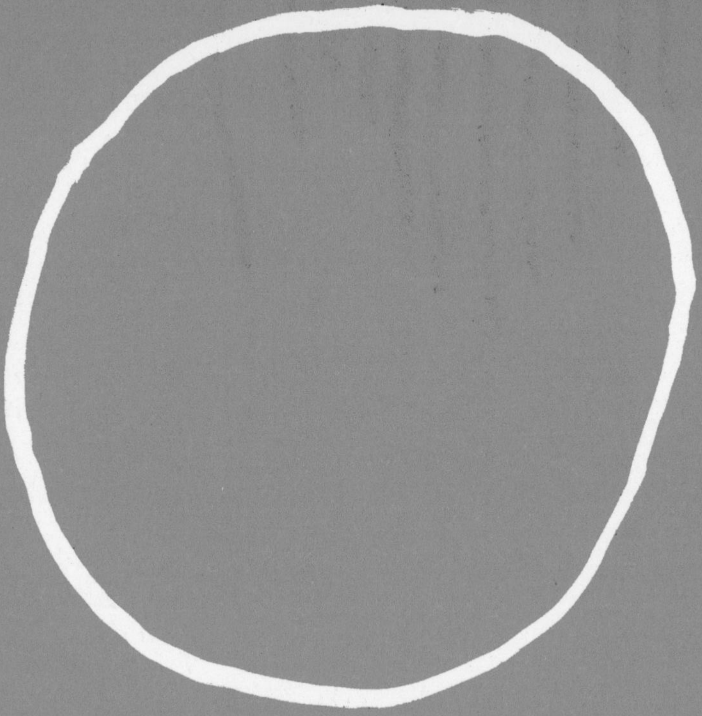

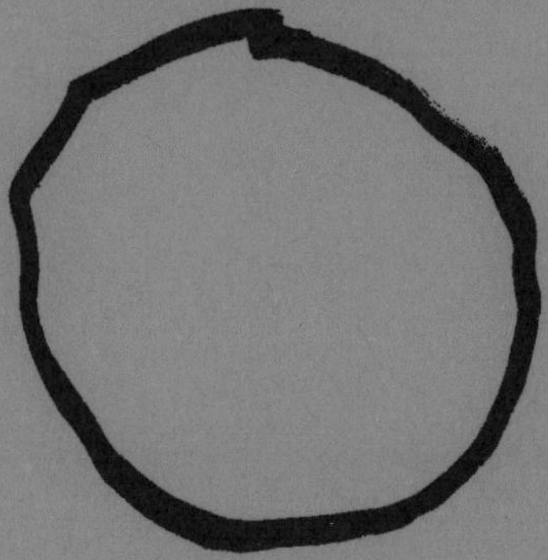

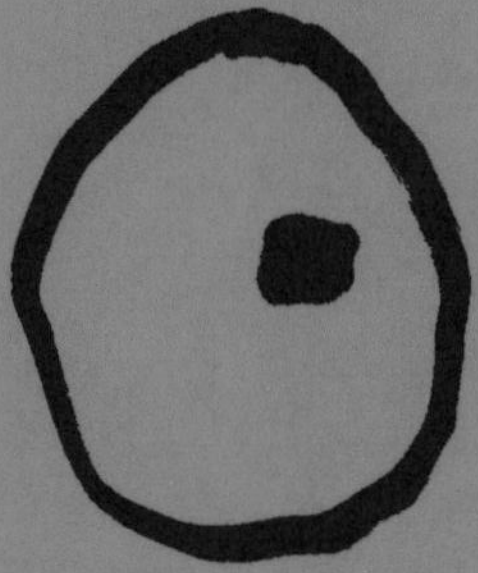

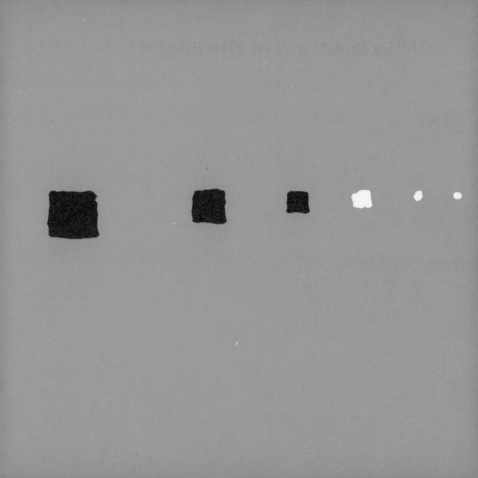

Who is sitting in the chairs?

What kind of fruits are these?

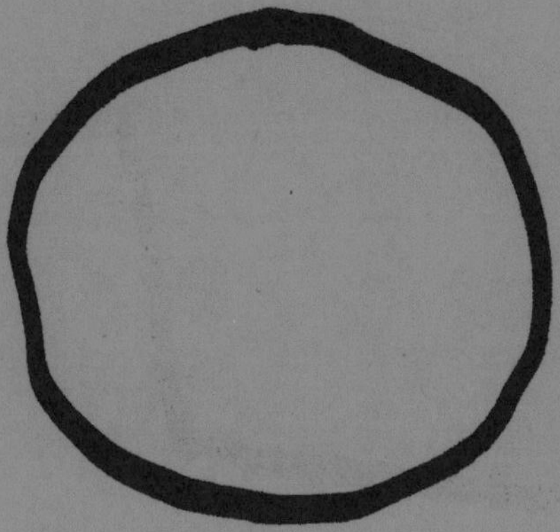

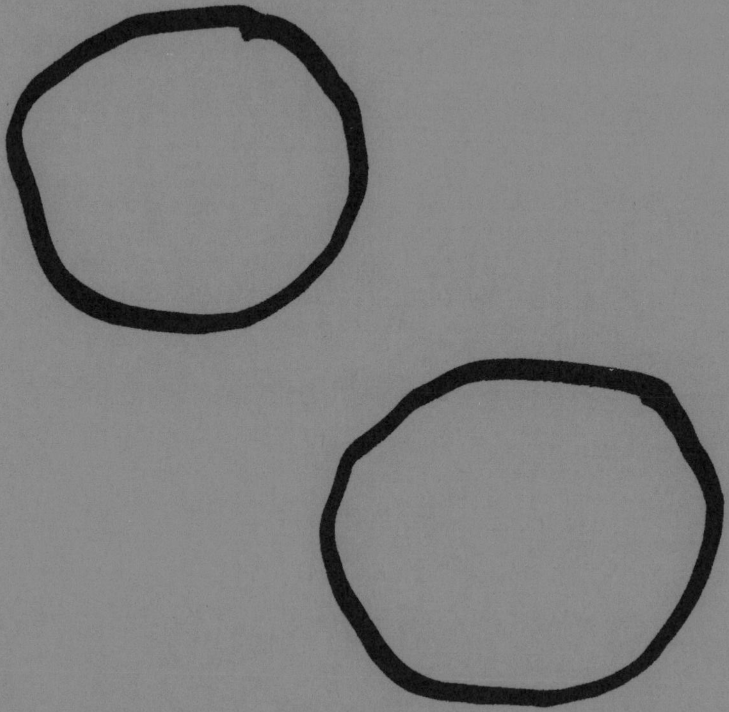

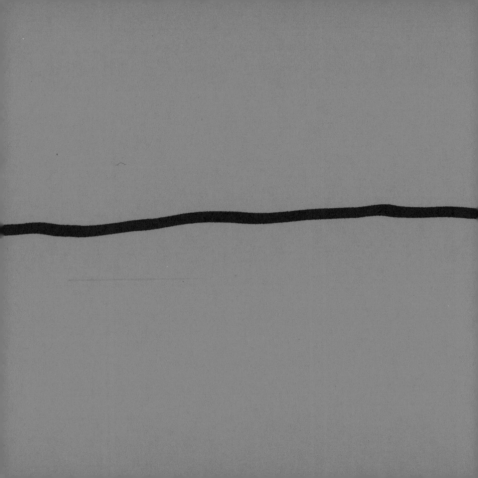

Are these candles?

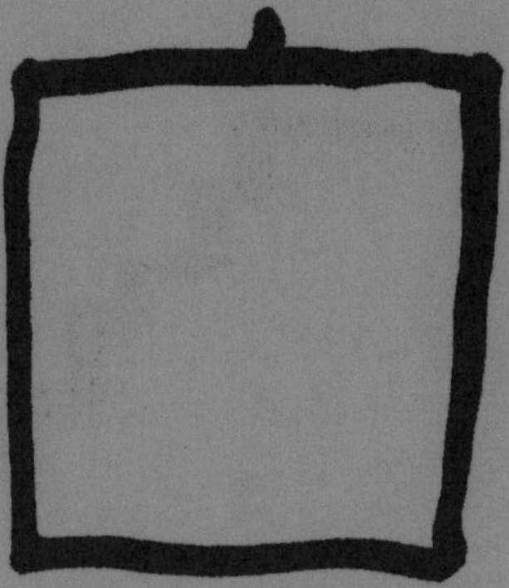

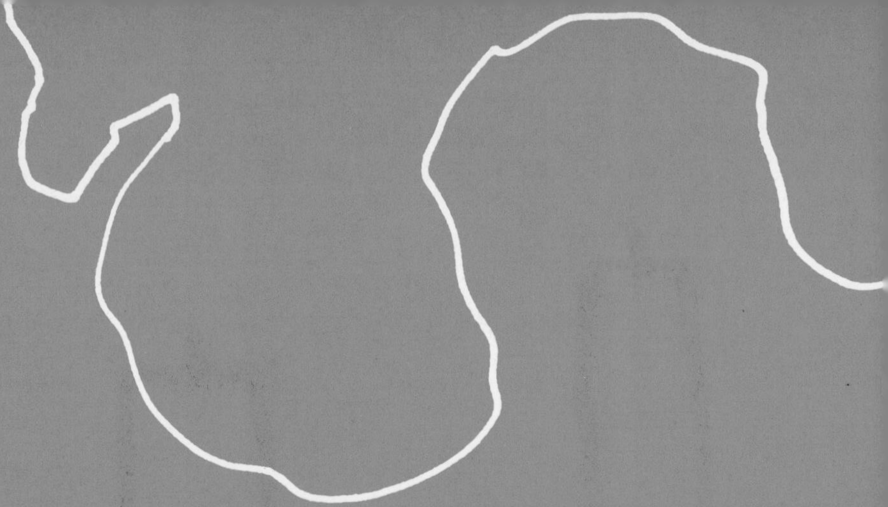

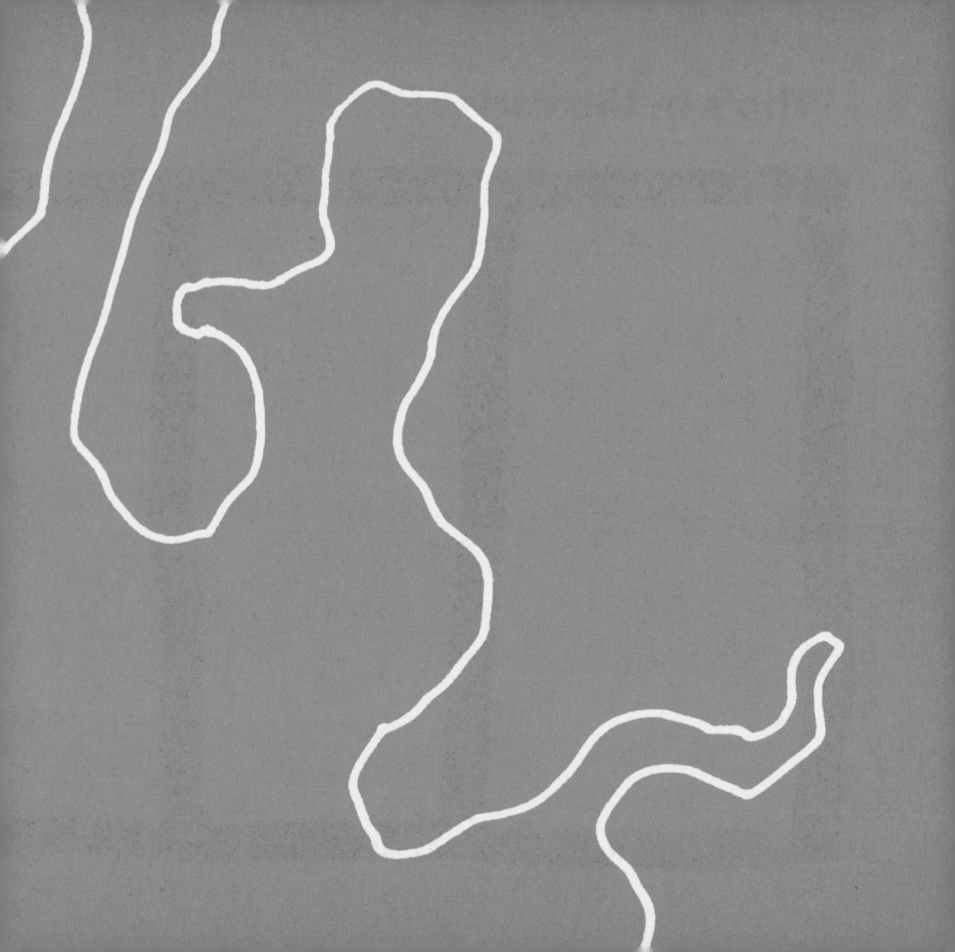

Who's in the cage?

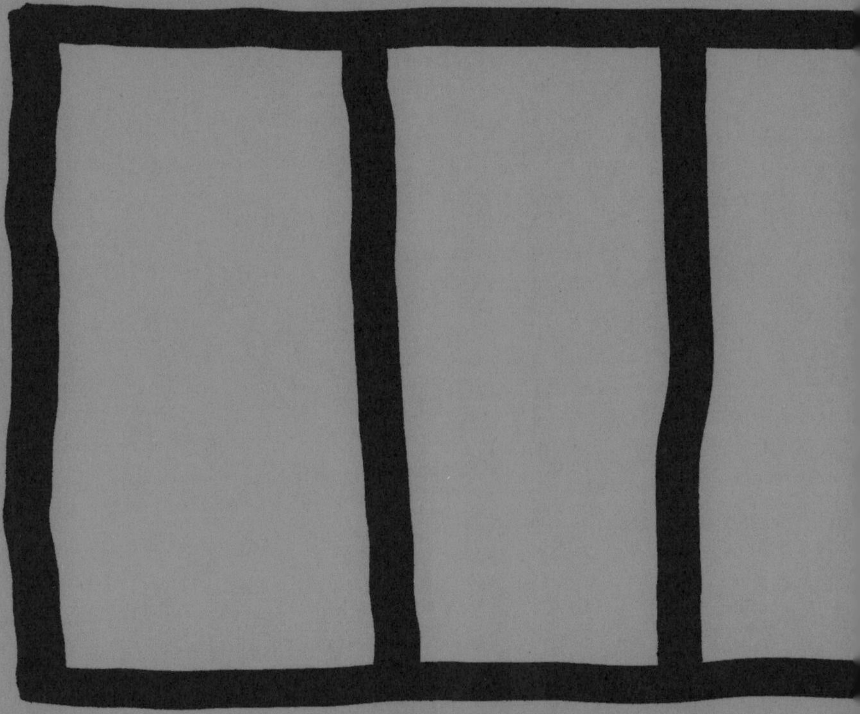

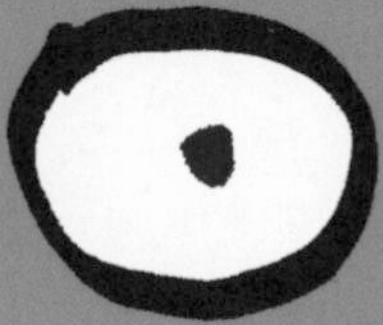

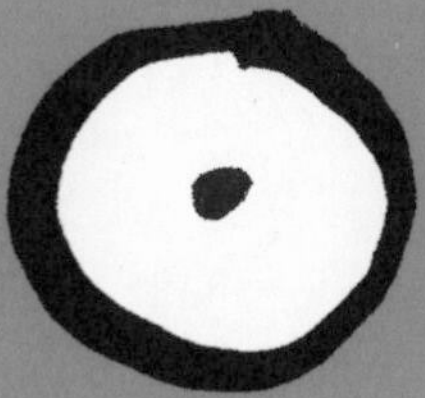

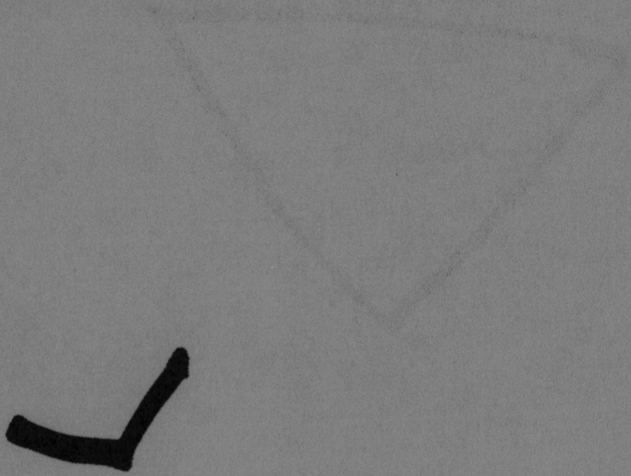

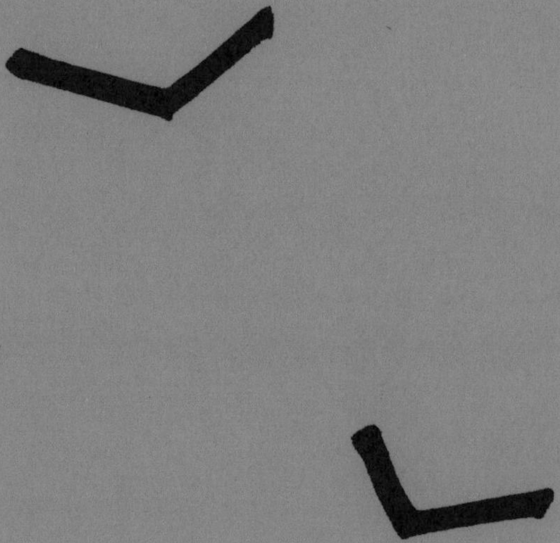

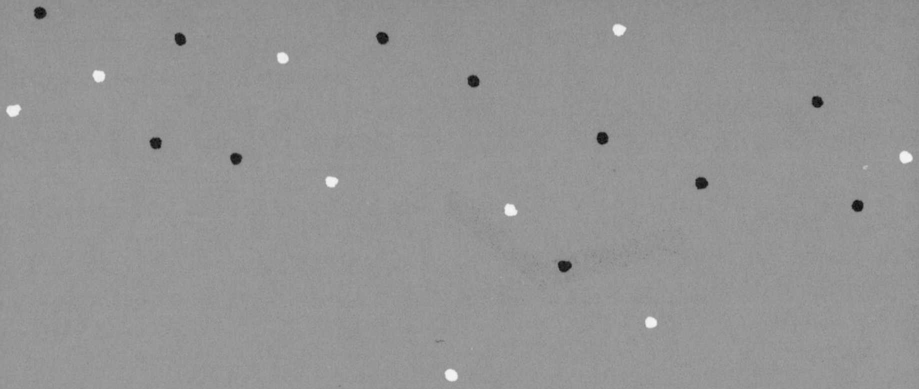

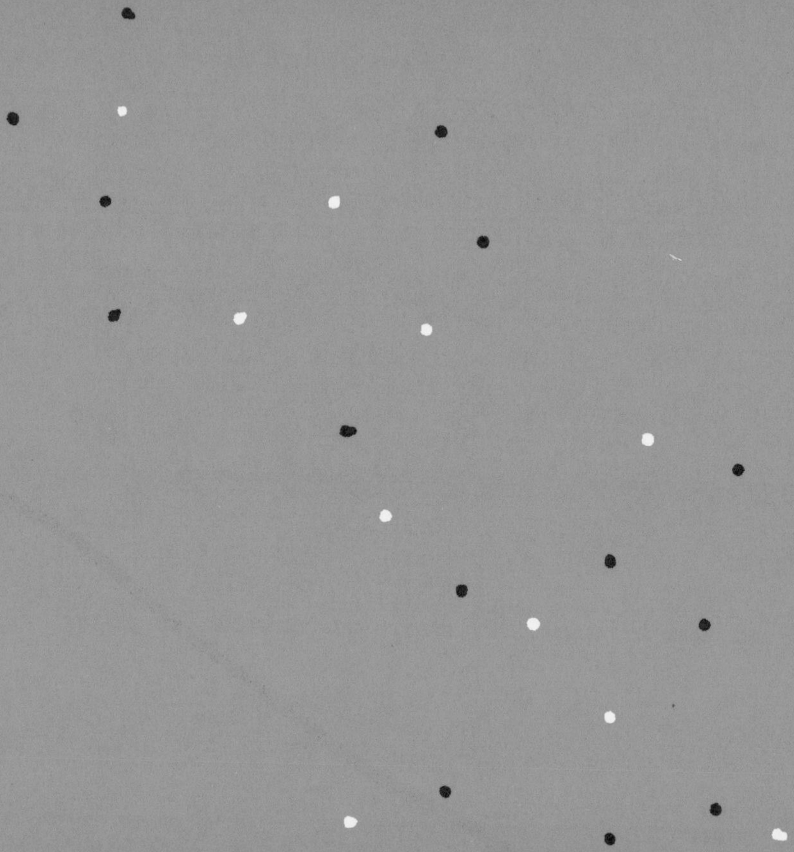

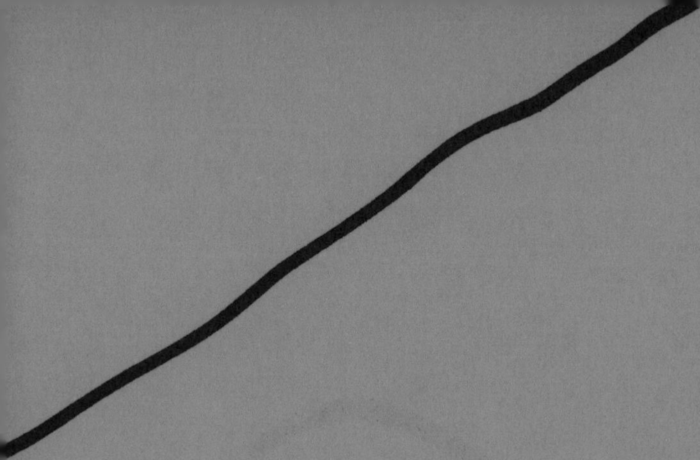

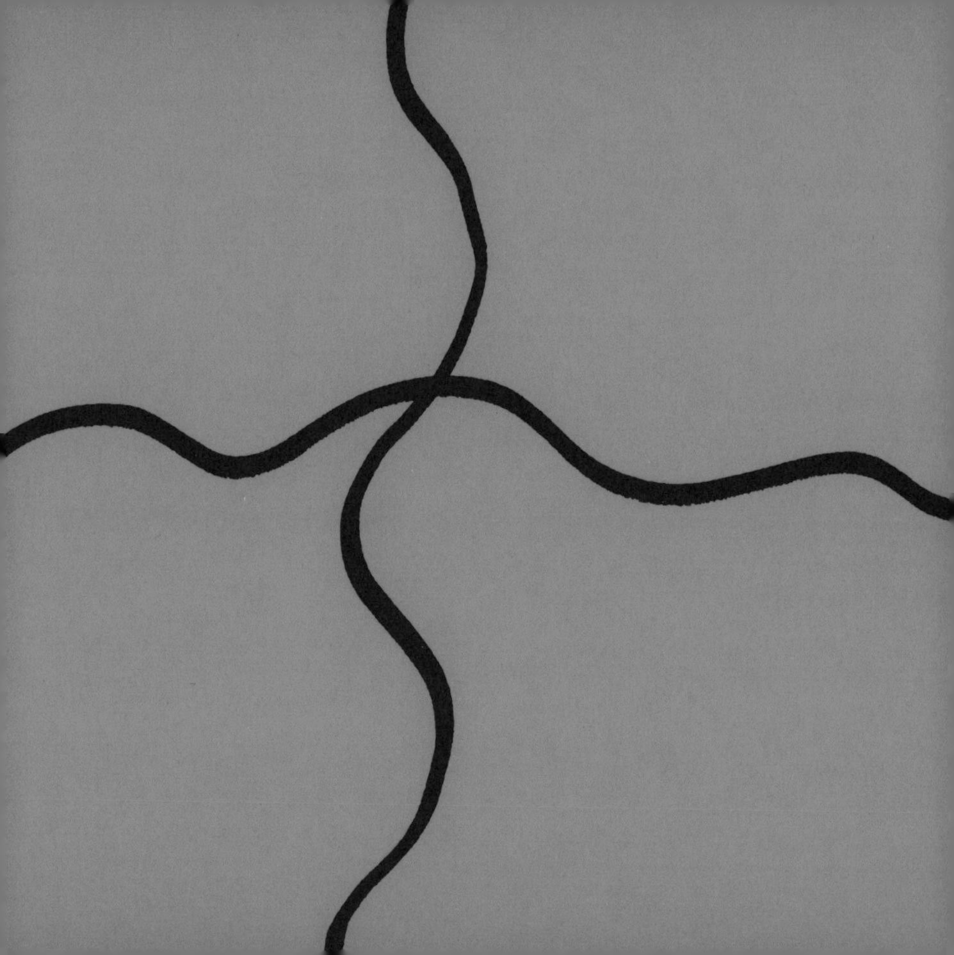

What time is it?

12
3
6
9

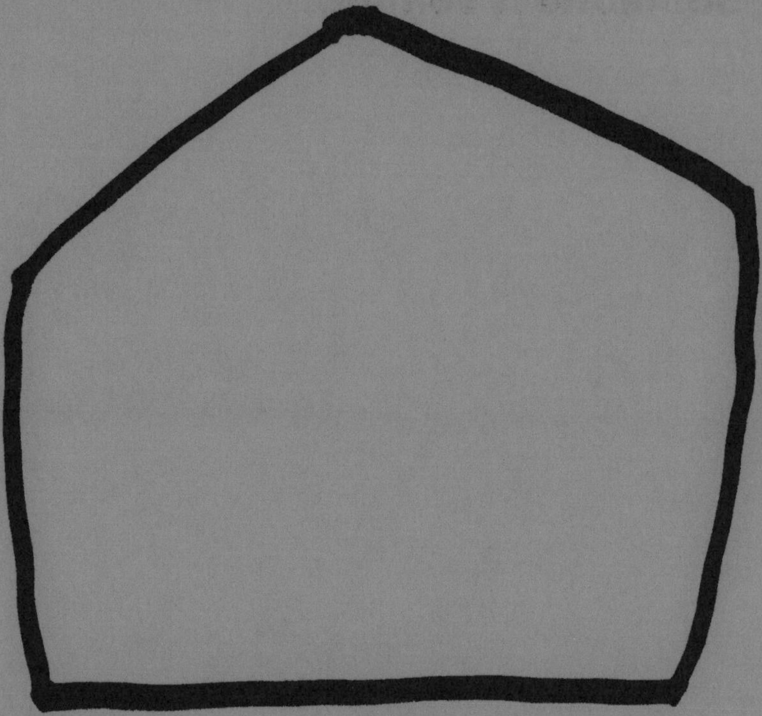

Someone is coming.

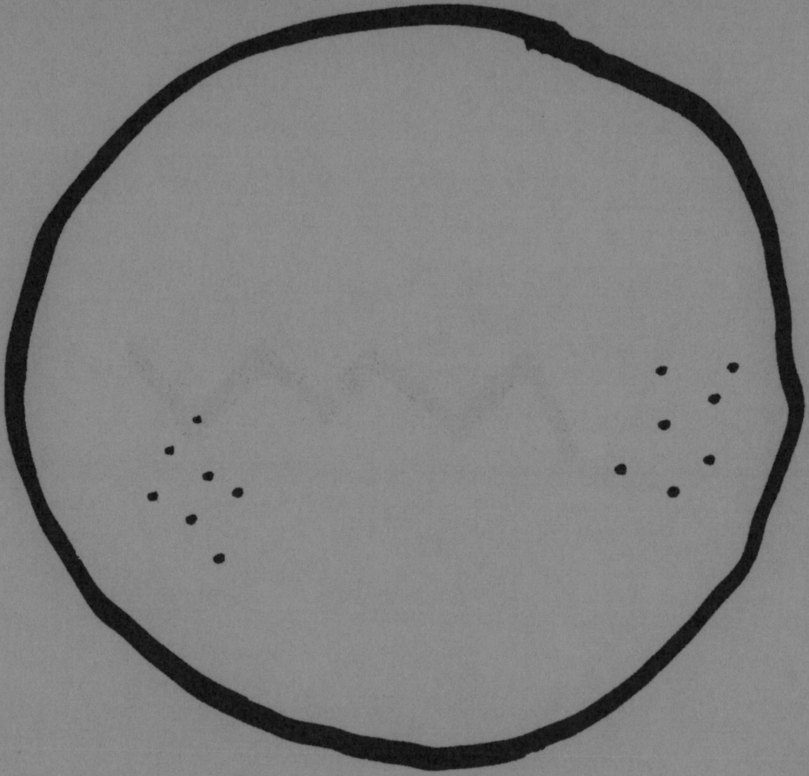

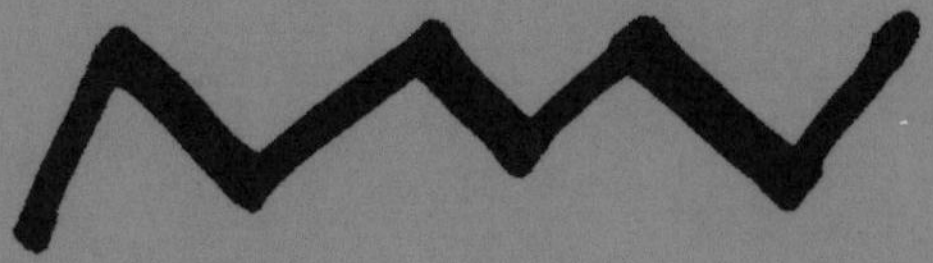

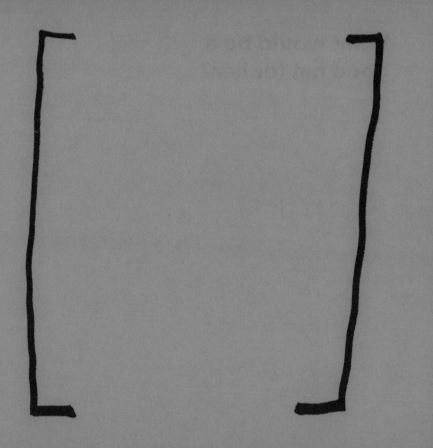

What would be a good hat for her?

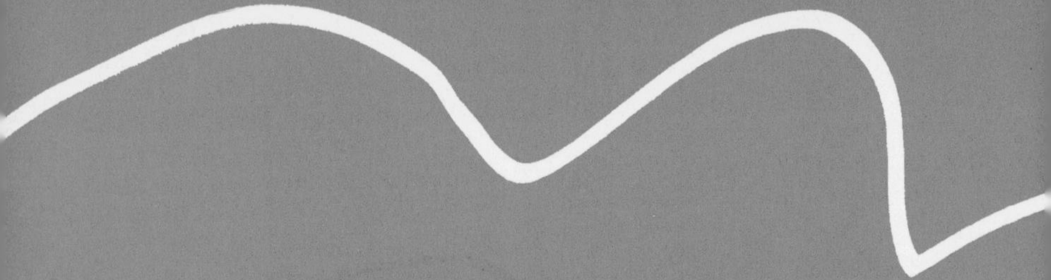

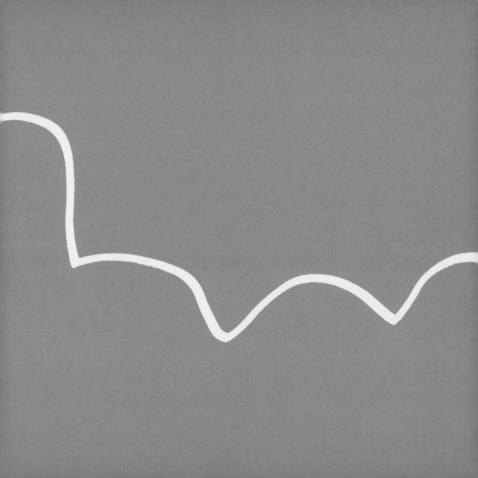

Who is in the car?

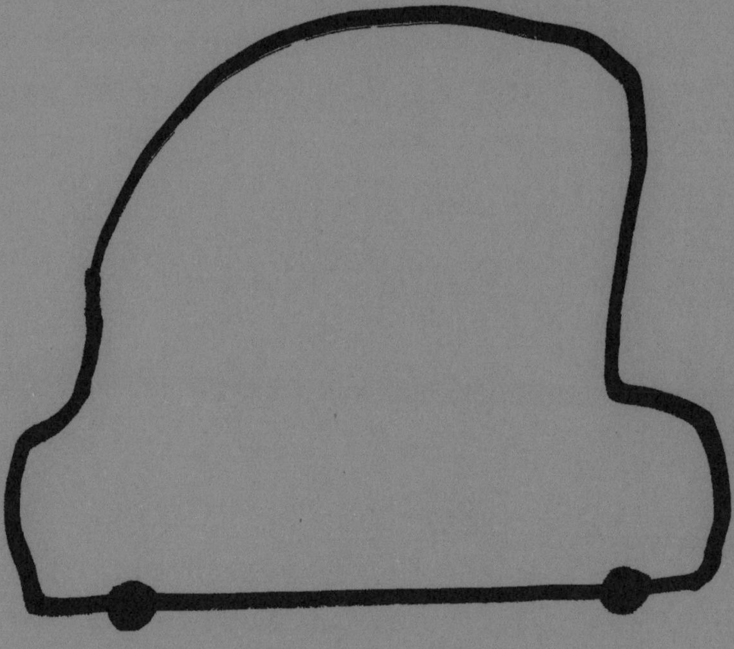

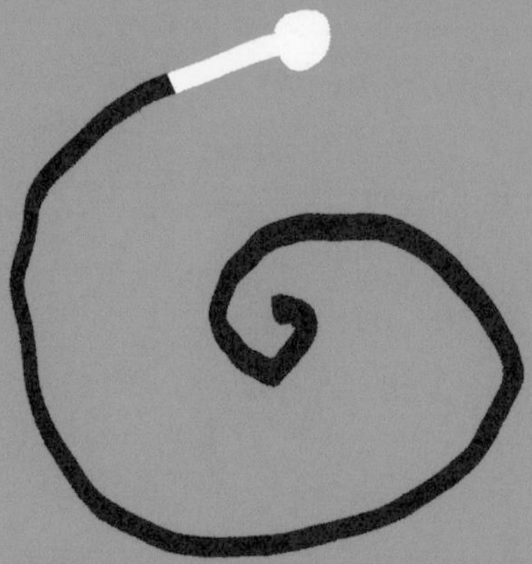

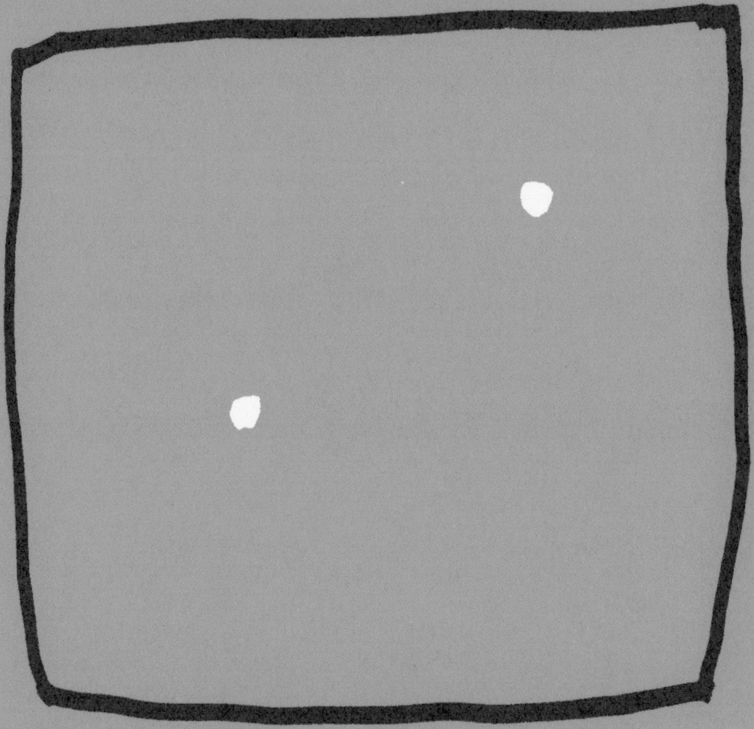

Oh, look, a shooting star!

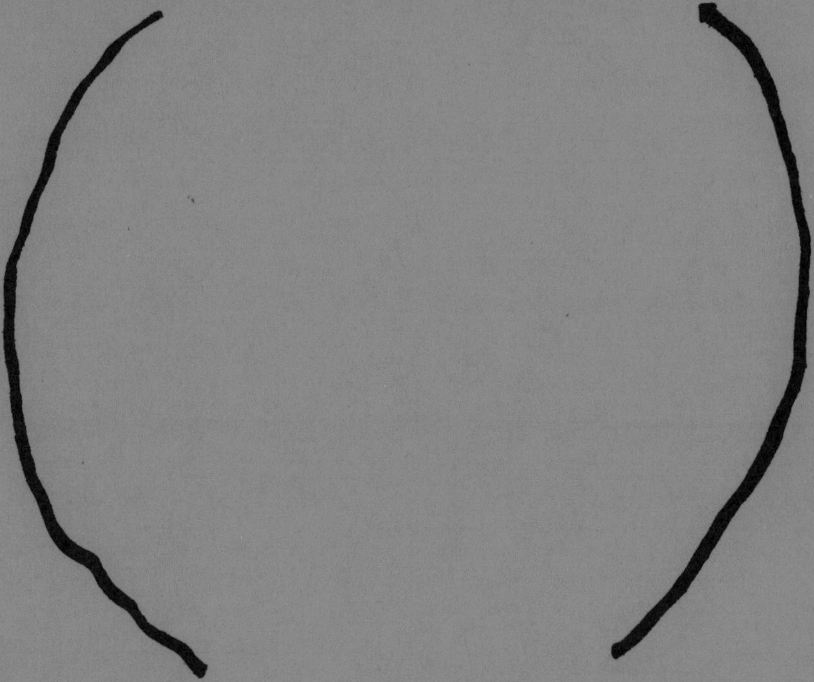

What kind of ice cream
is on the cone?

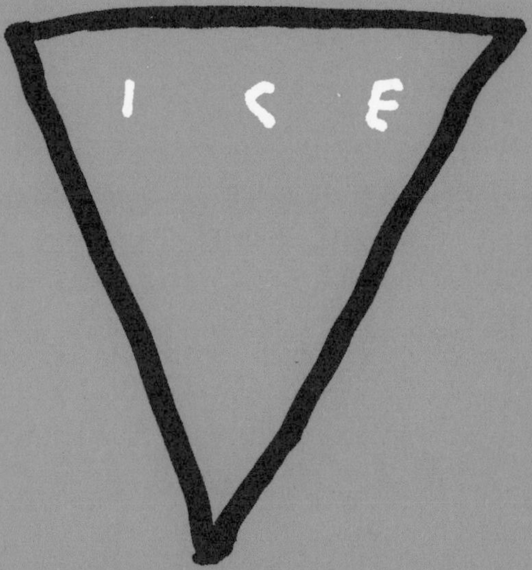
ICE

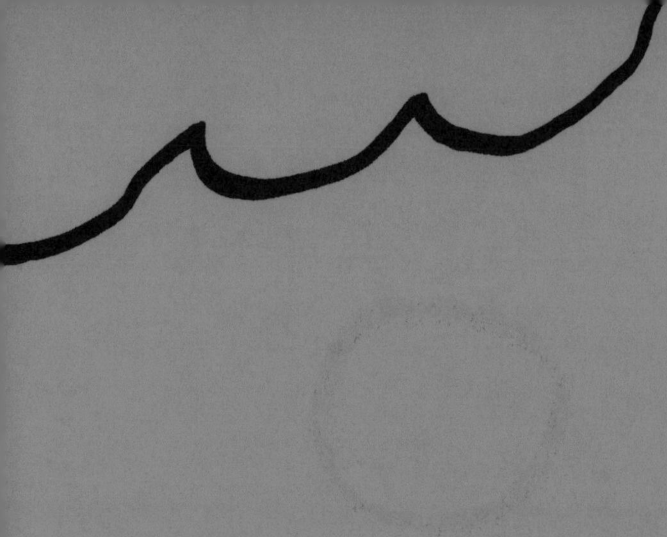

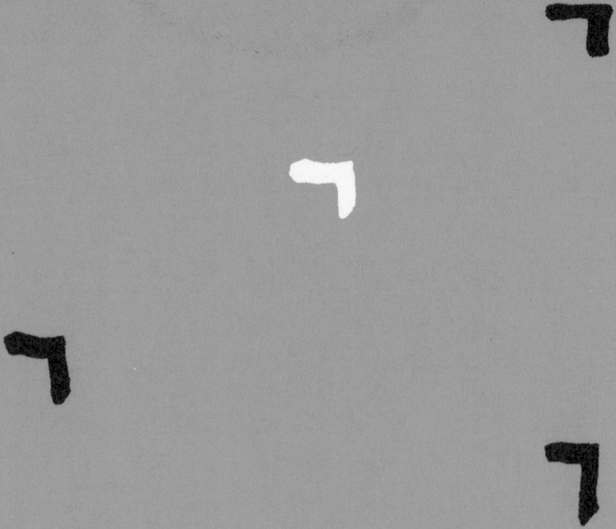

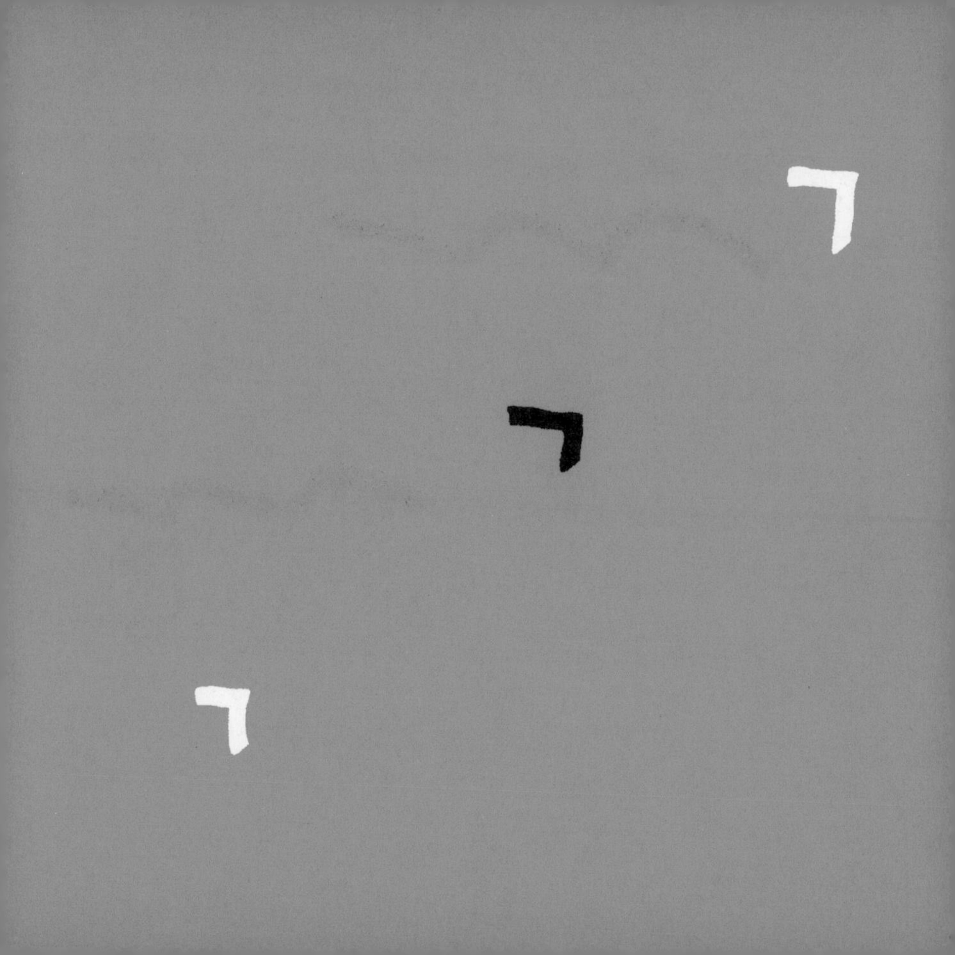

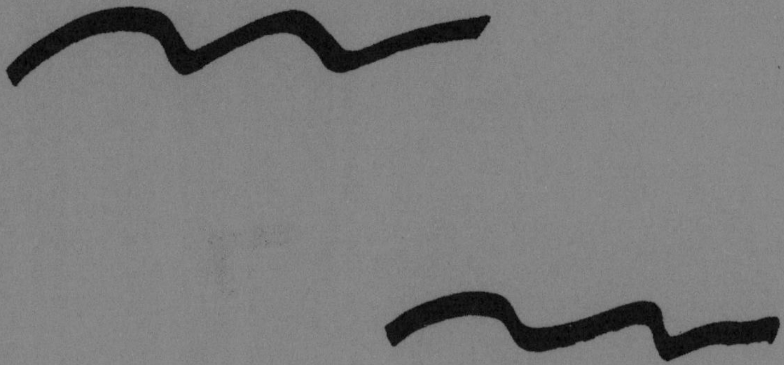

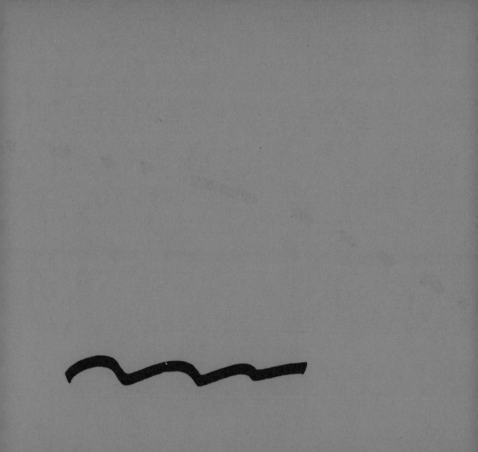

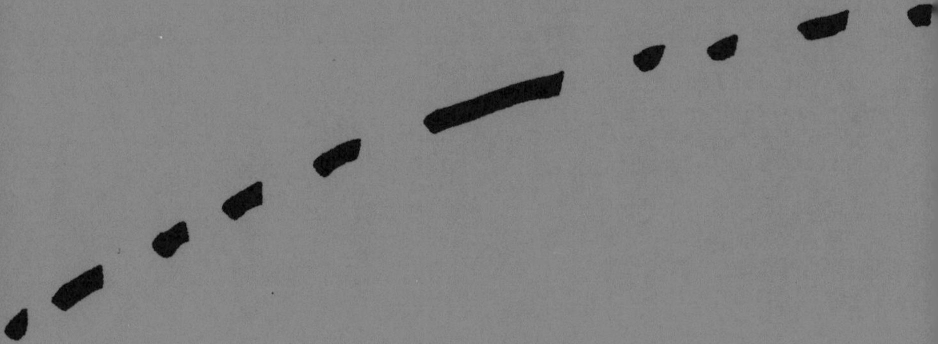

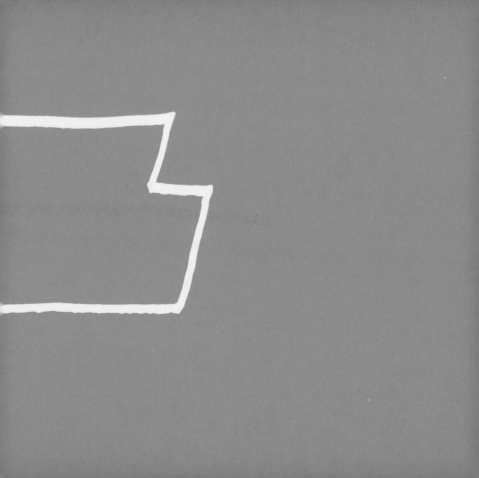

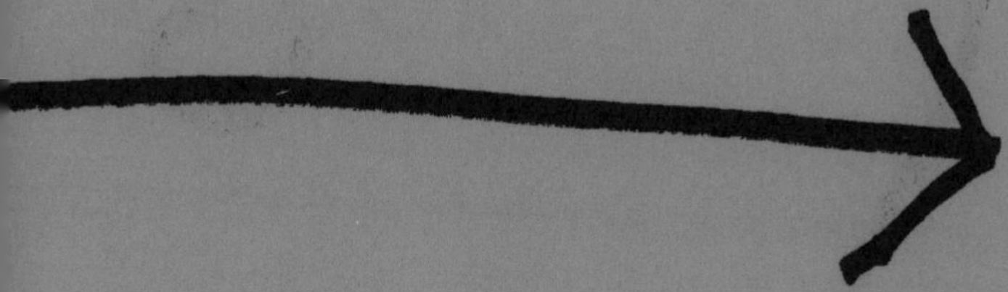

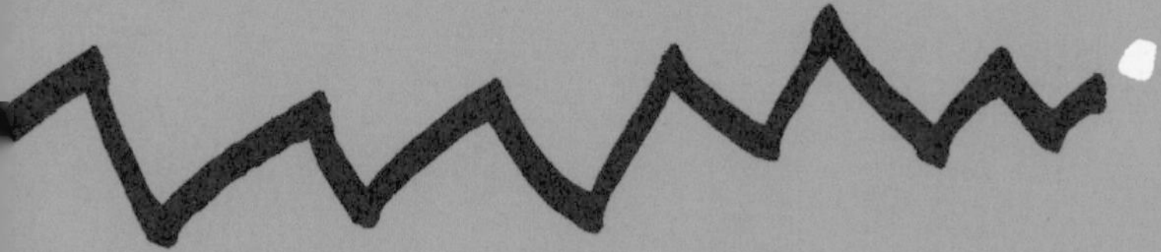

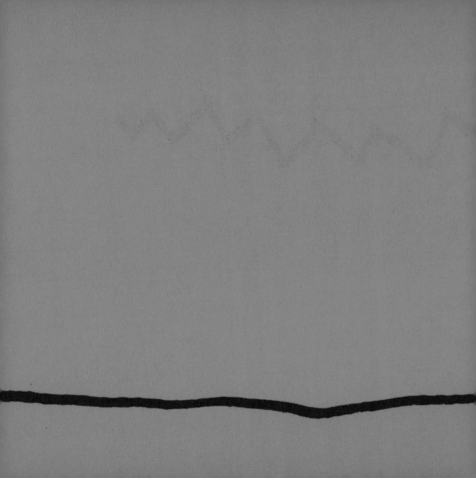

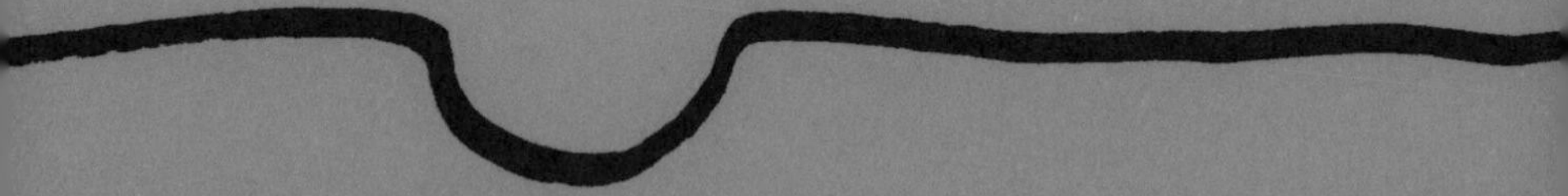

What's this?

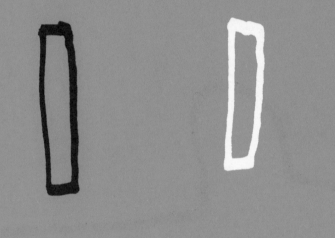

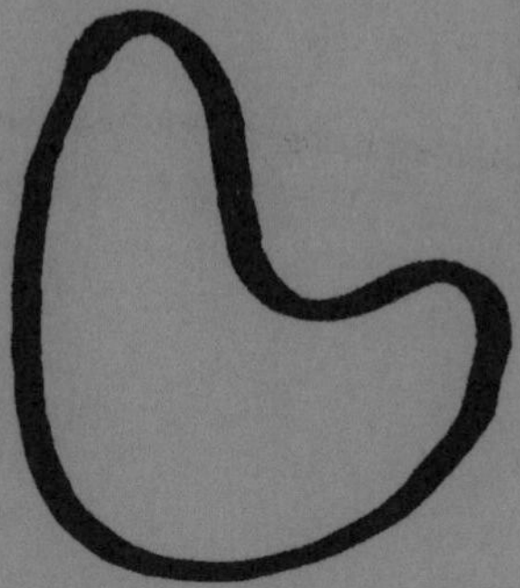

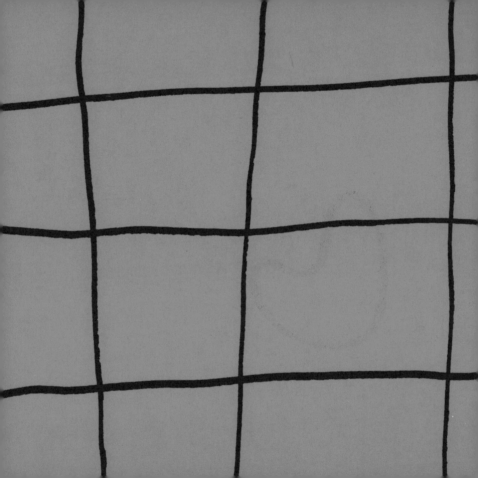

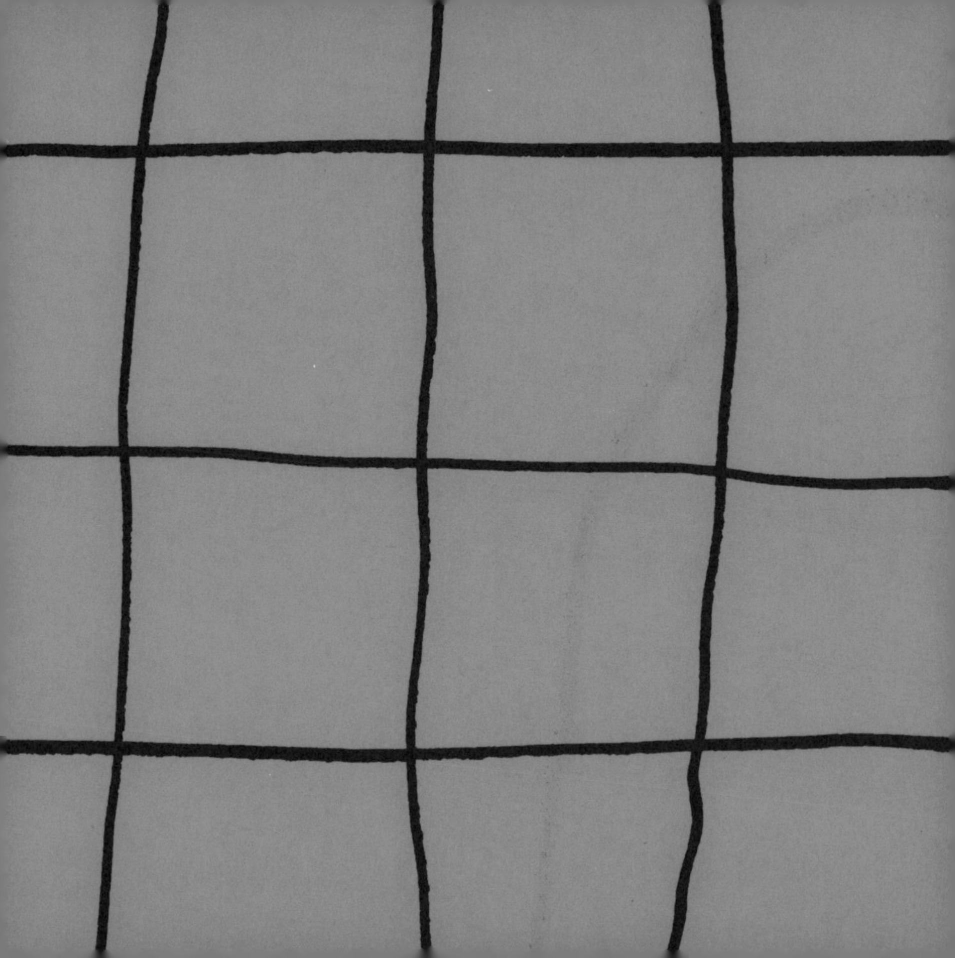

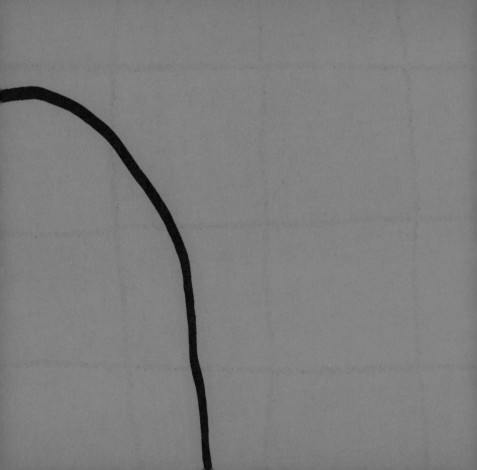

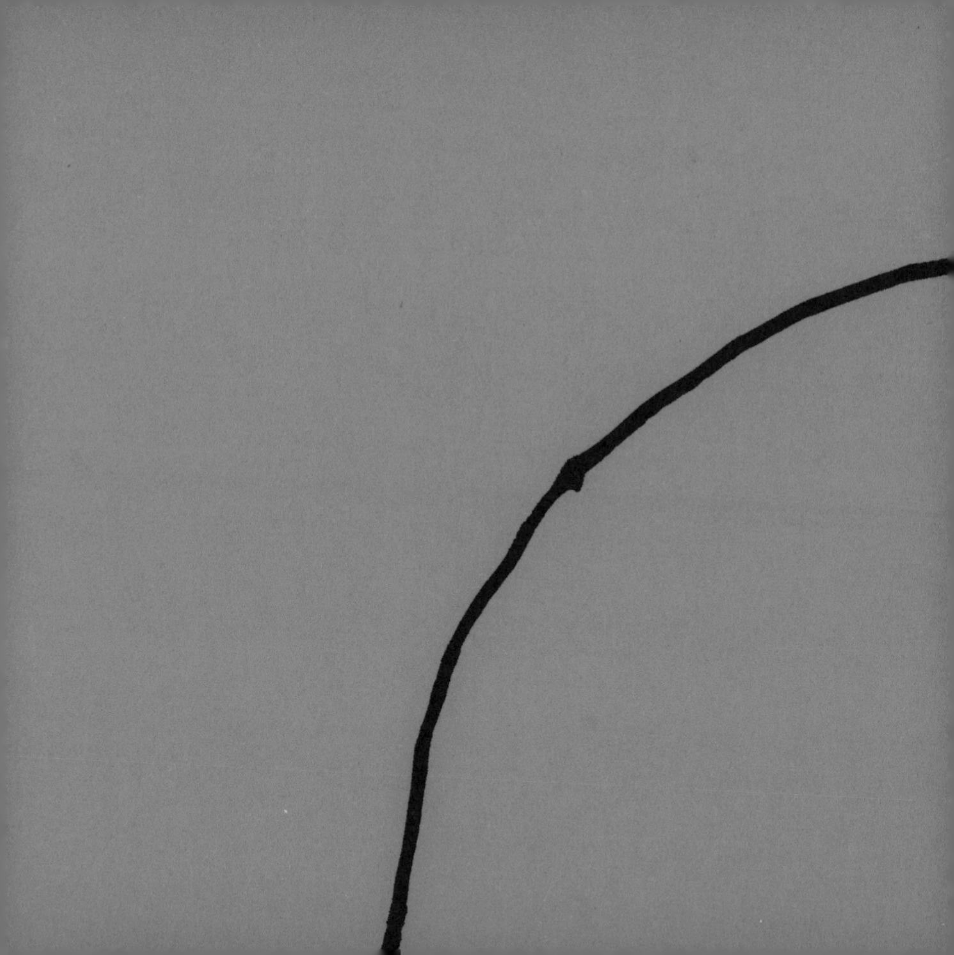

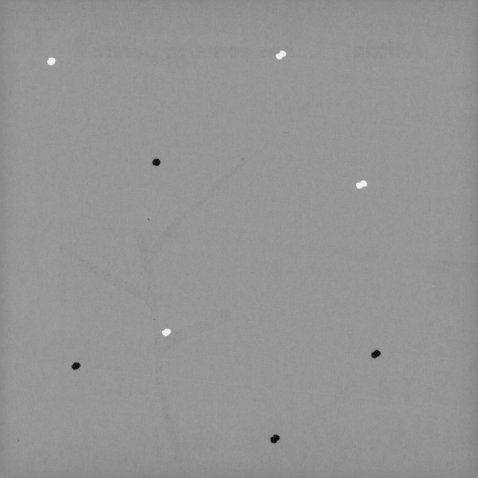

A little bird has come to perch.

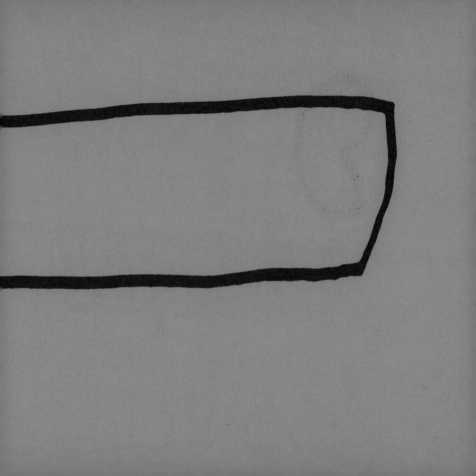

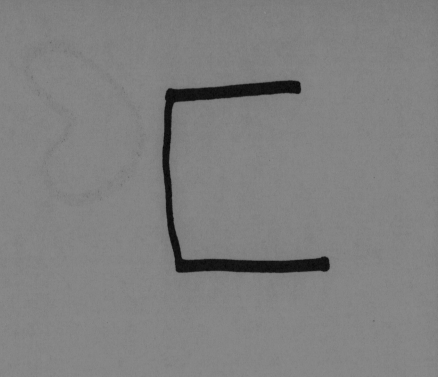

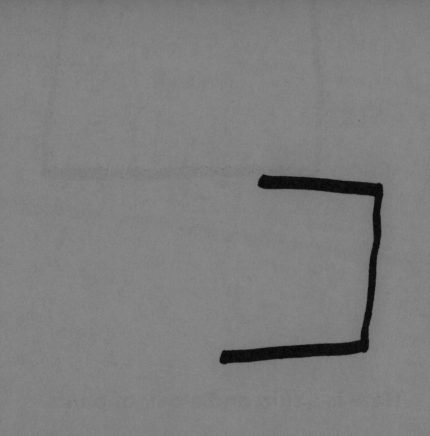

Here is a skirt and a pair of pants.

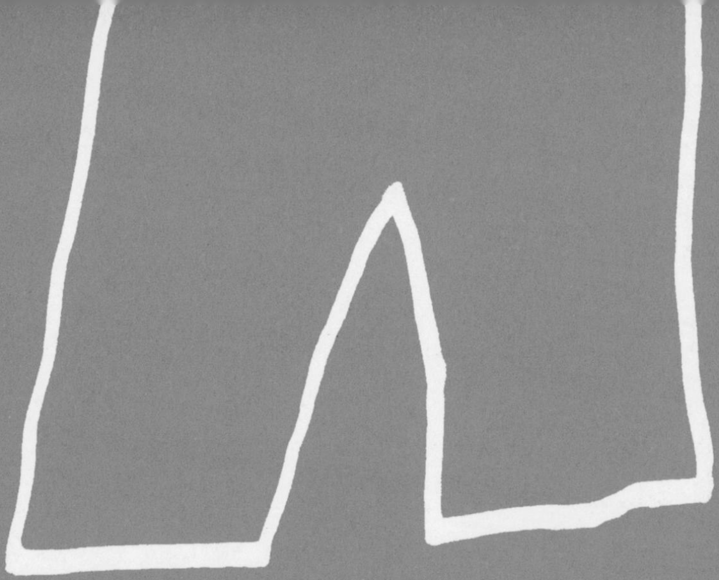

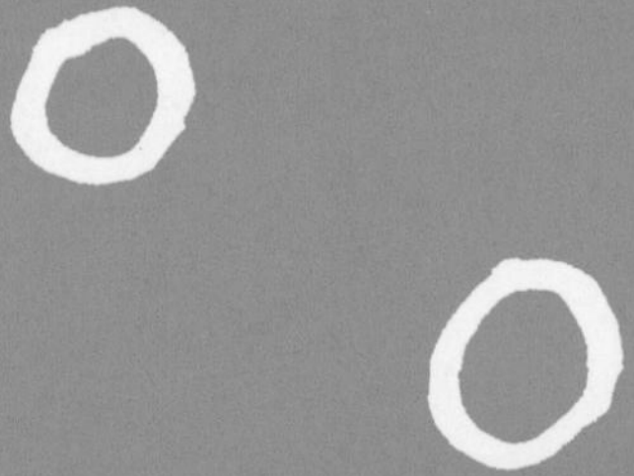

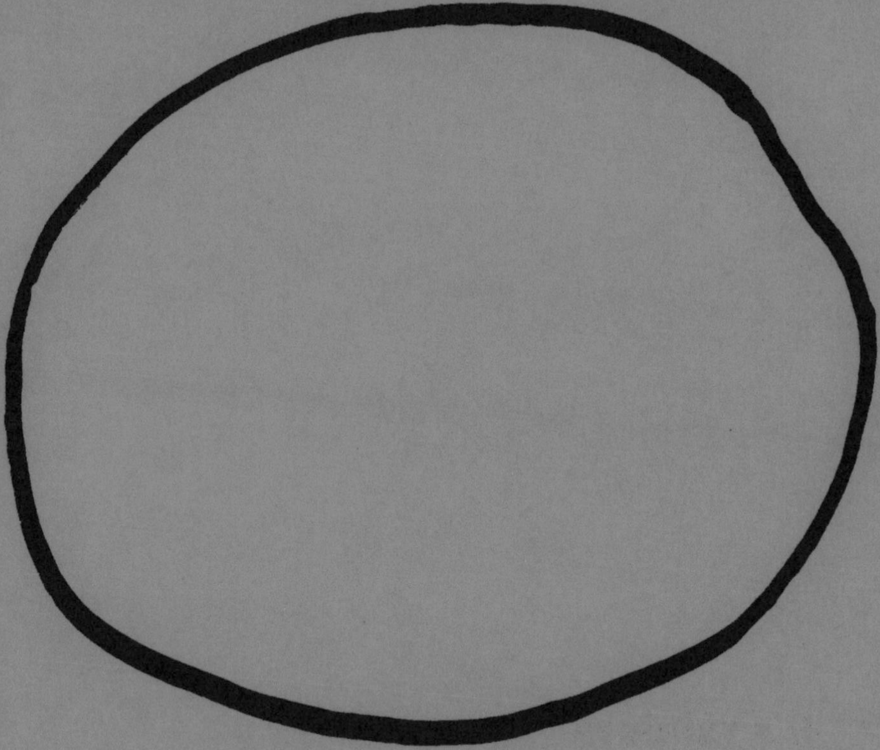

It’s raining!

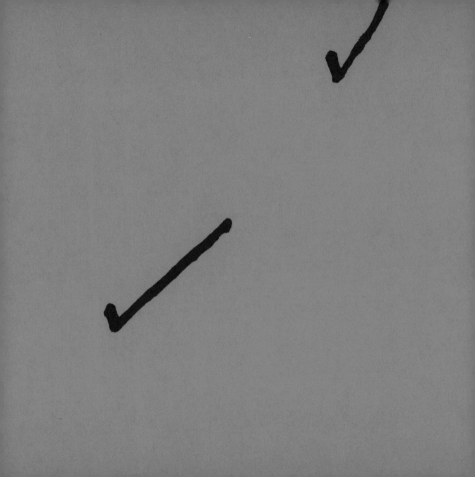

Who is swimming in the pool?

What are these shaggy things?

What’s this?

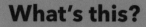

Friends!

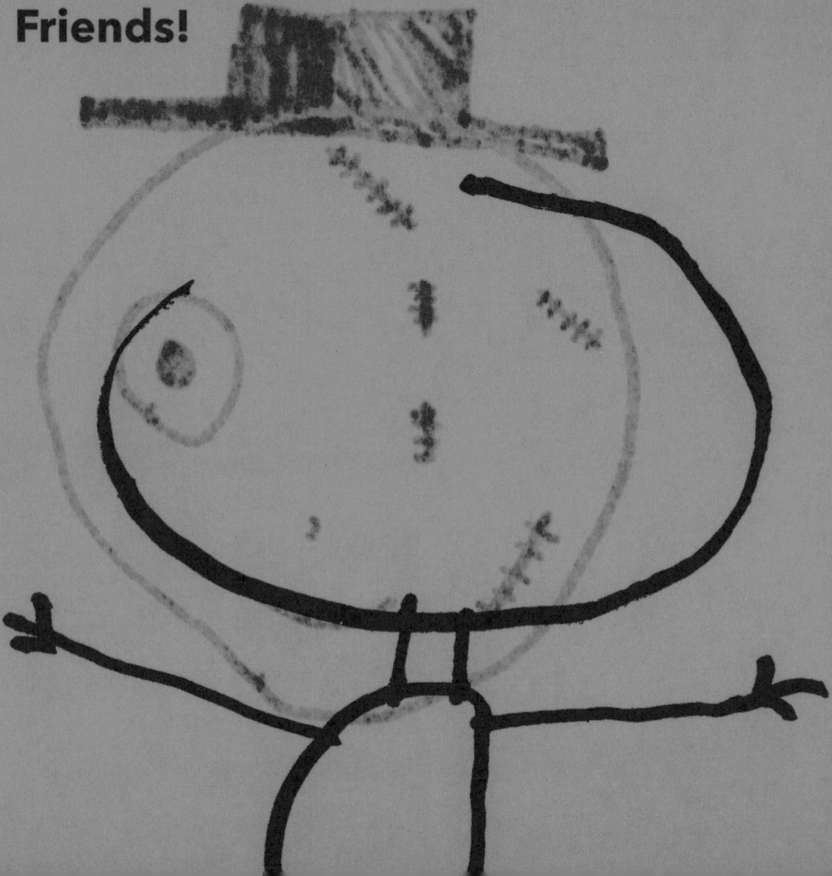

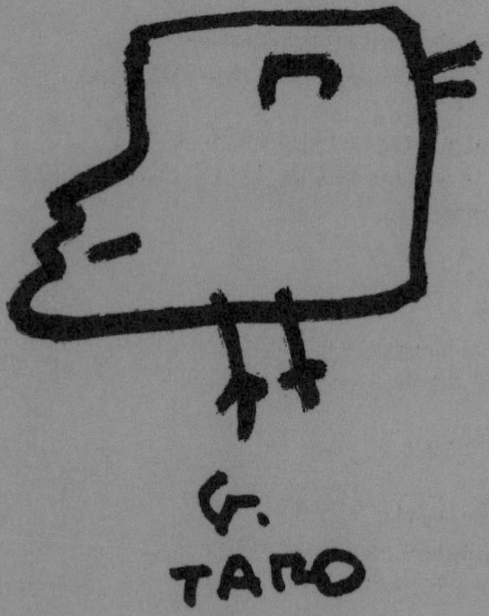

Doodling is always lots of fun. Let's doodle again!

Original edition published in Japan by BRONZE PUBLISHING Inc., Tokyo,
under the title *Okotta Tokino Rakugaki Book*.

First United States edition published in 2012 by Chronicle Books LLC.

ISBN 978-1-4521-0779-0

Manufactured in Singapore.
Typeset in Avenir.

1 3 5 7 9 10 8 6 4 2

Chronicle Books LLC
680 Second Street, San Francisco, California 94107
www.chroniclekids.com